A Little Bit

Married

A Little Bit
Married

How to Know When It's Time
to Walk Down the Aisle
or Out the Door

Hannah Seligson

Da Capo
LIFE
LONG

A Member of the Perseus Books Group

Interior design by Pauline Brown
Typeset in 11.75 point Fairfield Light

Library of Congress Cataloging-in-Publication Data

Seligson, Hannah.
A little bit married : how to know when it's time to walk down the aisle or out
the door / Hannah Seligson. — 1st ed.
    p. cm.
Includes bibliographical references.
ISBN 978-0-7382-1316-3 (alk. paper)
1. Unmarried couples. 2. Man-woman relationships. 3. Marriage. I. Title.
HQ803.5.S45 2009
646.7'7—dc22

2009026243

First Da Capo Press edition 2010

Published by Da Capo Press
A Member of the Perseus Books Group
www.dacapopress.com

Da Capo Press books are available at special discounts for bulk purchases in the
U.S. by corporations, institutions, and other organizations. For more information,
please contact the Special Markets Department at the Perseus Books Group,
2300 Chestnut Street, Suite 200, Philadelphia, PA 19103, or call
(800) 810-4145 extension 5000, or e-mail
special.markets@perseusbooks.com.

10 9 8 7 6 5 4 3 2 1

To my parents,
Judy Seligson and Allan Greenberg.

Contents

Introduction

> In our imperfectly organised society there is no provision as yet for the young woman who claims the privileges of marriage without assuming its obligations.
>
> —*The House of Mirth*, Edith Wharton

It was somewhere between the baked ziti he made for me one very cold Tuesday night in November and a ski trip we took in January when I fell in love with Daniel. We were seniors in college, but this wasn't the era of free love or part of the casual hook-up culture that has recently come in vogue. Daniel took me home to meet his parents, grandparents, and cousins. Seamlessly we became part of each other's lives. His Mom used to ask when we would have children. Although marriage never came up explicitly, the signs that I imagined were culminating into making a life-long commitment were everywhere. Very quickly—between the ziti and the ski trip—Daniel told me he loved me. I had received a job offer in New York, and Daniel quickly accepted one as well. Our lives were moving in sync.

In late June of 2004, after graduation, we moved to New York. We didn't officially live together, but my apartment became a very expensive closet. I spent the majority of the week at Daniel's apartment, fully cementing our domestic routine: ordering in sesame chicken and scallion pancakes from Grand Sichuan and watching *Hardball*.

In hindsight, of course, I can appreciate that my view of the relationship was rather myopic. I was deeply embedded. Daniel and I were playing house. But that makes it sound like some charade. We were doing things that, in any other era, would have been considered a direct pathway to marriage. Today, it's just considered practice or, as I came to call it, being A Little Bit Married. The vacations we took together, the enormous amount of time we spent with each other's families, and the daily emotional binding and sacrifices we made for each other read—for me—as a tacit agreement that we'd do this for a few years and then get married. In my mind, there was no other interpretation. Daniel, however, ultimately did have a very different interpretation. His doubts reached a boiling point the following June. For him, there was some abstract notion of love and commitment that our relationship wasn't meeting. It's been said that his breakup reasoning about not wanting to spend all of his money in his bank account on me and that "we don't stay up talking on the phone until 2 AM" were plucked directly from an episode of *Dawson's Creek*.

Although at the time my breakup with Daniel felt like the most personal painful experience, it was a relationship rite of passage that the vast majority of young people today will go through. This book is an attempt to understand the atmospherics of "A Little Bit Married" as a new relationship ritual. Why are people not only dating for such long periods of time, but also making marriage-like sacrifices when they aren't married? When is the breaking point for those of us who are A Little Bit Married? Is it after six months? A year? Three years? The one universal rule that does apply is that relationships need momentum, and a point in the future can help build and sustain that momentum. After that initial haze of falling in love, which has a shelf life of about six months, there will inevitably be questions about the future—whether it's after a year and a half and your boyfriend casually mentions he would like to move to London for a few years, or it's after five years and you decide to take that film job in Los Angeles that you've been dreaming about since college.

The dating landscape is now teeming with e-mail queries like this one: "Hello, my girlfriend and I are in search of a one bedroom apartment on the East Side." Girlfriend, I wondered? Maybe he meant fiancée? I tried to construct their life story for a moment. He must be in his mid-thirties and getting ready to pop the question, but wants to try it out before he makes a commitment that today could easily last fifty years. I scrolled down to the bottom of his e-mail. He graduated in 2005, which, by my best estimation, put him at twenty-four years old—and he was moving in with his girlfriend.

In cities across America, apartments are littered with specimens that, even forty years ago, anthropologists would have said confirmed that a couple lived there as husband and wife. "Yeah, I lost a good half of my wardrobe and a couple hundred dollars in gadgets," Evan, twenty-nine, said about the belongings that are now in the abyss of "things that now belong to my ex" after his relationship with his live-in girlfriend of three years petered out. Peek into the condos and homes of most twenty-something couples in a relationship today and, if they haven't moved in officially, it sure looks like they have. Their belongings—toothbrushes, T-shirts, and iPods—will one day be considered artifacts of the early days of the twenty-first-century romantic rite of passage: the long-term relationship. Somewhere in between the commonly recognized romantic rites of passages—your first kiss, your first boyfriend or girlfriend, losing your virginity, and, of course, marriage—you now get your marriage training wheels with your first mini-marriage.

How can you be A Little Bit Married? Isn't that as oxymoronic as saying someone is a little bit pregnant? You would think. After interviewing over one hundred men and women who have spent at least a year in a monogamous relationship, "A Little Bit Married" was the only way to define this pervasive relationship state. These are relationships that even sixty or seventy years ago would have most likely culminated in marriage, but, because of a host of social, economic, and cultural factors that I'll discuss in greater detail throughout this book, often do not. Although a year was the qualifying length of time to be considered "A Little Bit Married," over half the people interviewed for this book had been dating for over two years.

An important disclaimer before we continue: The research and reporting I did for this book focuses on a small slice of the social pie. The interviewees were mostly upwardly mobile, college-educated twenty- and thirty-somethings living in urban areas. In other pockets of the country, there is a much different relationship landscape—namely the trend of marrying very early. And in other parts of the globe, like in many European countries, young people are brushing off marriage altogether. This book is not meant as a grandiose romantic state of the union. Rather, its goal is to sketch out what's happening among people who are A Little Bit Married—a population that does not represent the socio-economic or psychographic dimensions of everyone in this cohort.

If A Little Bit Married had an avatar, it would be Prince William, heir to the British throne, and his girlfriend, Kate Middleton, who have been dating for over six years. Although Britain's betting shops put the odds on a 2009 marriage at 2:1,[1] there has been no official royal press release about an upcoming engagement, bucketing them in with the millions of other couples who are just A Little Bit Married. The snarky British tabloids even dubbed her "Waitie Katie." Meanwhile, on the other side of the Atlantic, I witnessed just about every friend and friend's friend drift in and out of long-term relationships. It was everywhere I looked. That became the impetus to take the conversations from informal (you know, the ones at the brunch table about whether he should take the plunge and propose or the half-lucid mea culpa of "we are living together, but I'll never marry someone who isn't Jewish") to a formal interview process. I had some loosely formed theories based on the dozens of hours I'd spent mulling over the question that was at the crux of these relationships: How do you know when it's time to end the rehearsal and either walk down the aisle or out the door? The axis many of these mock marriages turned on was the looming question, "Do I want to marry this person?" A question that, for many A Little Bit Marrieds, takes years of rehearsal to answer.

To begin mining for answers, I had to examine what these relationships looked like in the flesh and blood, from both the male and female perspective. Were these long-term relationships different for men and women? Did these couples talk about marriage? Why were men and women staying in relationships for half of their twenties or well into their thirties if they weren't going to marry the person? What were they hoping to discover about their partner in these prolonged years of dating? Were women of Generation Y conforming to the stereotypes of women chomping at the bit to get married while their boyfriends preferred to remain bachelors? Or was this generation turning that gender dynamic on its head? What were the challenges and benefits of being A Little Bit Married? The reporting process gave me a high-focus lens into the marital aspirations as well as romantic desires and fears of my generation. In order to sociologically and psychologically contextualize this new romantic rite of passage, the book includes insights from psychologists, sociologists, anthropologists, and relationship experts.

In the ensuing chapters, I'll go into much greater detail about the many facets of being A Little Married, exploring everything from career trade-offs couples make to be in these relationships, to whether men and women view their marriage timetables differently, to what effect today's prolonged adolescence has on our marital ambitions and whether the fear of the dating trenches keeps us A Little Bit Married long past the relationship's expiration date, to what qualities people look for during these years of courtship.

But, for a moment, I will talk in broad strokes about what these relationships, in their best form, offer. Yes, many do not pan out to proffer life-long compatibility or children, but they do, on the other hand, tender a great learning experience, valuable ego-building, a stay against loneliness, and some lessons about how to act or not to act in a relationship. For example, Kate, twenty-seven, now single, described it like this: "Being a little married is like what I would imagine being married is like—sometimes it sucks and sometimes it's great. It's cool being in love and fantasizing and planning for the future. It's great not to be lonely. On the flip side, it sucks to question the character/intentions/body odor/overall compatibility of the person you are spending almost all of your free time with, and you've gotten yourself all occupied while something better could be behind you." Maya, twenty-seven, who has been in and out of her long-term relationship for eight years, says: "You get to see what life would be like—it's like an internship. Look, families and relationships are complicated, so it gives you a window into whether you want this for the rest of your life."

1
First Comes Love, Then Comes A Little Bit Married

Why the Long-Term Relationship
Has Become the New
Romantic Rite of Passage

> Dating is not what it was fifty years ago. Dating is evolving into this gradual process of moving in. It involves nights spent over at one or the other's place. There's the toothbrush, then a few items of clothing. All of a sudden, they realize they've moved in.
>
> —Pamela Smock, University of Michigan
> Institute for Social Research

"So, catch me up. What's going on with school? Your love life?" I asked my friend Sara at our monthly girls' night in. "School is fine," she said, glossing over the details to get to what she really wanted to talk about: her relationship. "But I'm in a stalemate with Adam," she confided. Her boyfriend of over a year had just dropped the bomb that he wasn't sure if he was ready to get married. She told us, "He says he is waiting for some sign that this is right. I'm twenty-five and he is twenty-seven, shouldn't we be moving toward

marriage? And now do I just wait around for him to be ready? My time is valuable." Right, in other centuries women gave their virginity, now the equivalent is our time. The room fell silent as everyone channeled some version of their own current or past "Adam" situation.

My grandparents went on five dates over a ten-month period before my grandfather proposed. They were happily married for forty-seven years. Nowadays, five dates is the point when you've friended each other on Facebook and are in the midst of a series of coy e-mail and text-message exchanges. The era in which my grandparents courted was defined by a compressed time frame—everything happened very fast. It's the opposite today; the courtship and dating rituals have been elongated. In another not-so-distant time, to even sleep in the same bed—let alone live together as a couple—was considered an unspoken agreement to get married. But today, as Evan, twenty-nine, who has been dating his girlfriend for six years, puts it, "You can start your life without a gold band on your finger." Marriage is no longer the big bang it was for earlier generations. There is now a huge stopgap between dating and marriage—it's a place where young men and women are forming long-term relationships that have many similarities to marriage, yet aren't quite. Welcome to the age of A Little Bit Married.

The Odyssey Years

In a widely circulated piece, "The Odyssey Years," David Brooks, an op-ed columnist at the *New York Times*, recently pondered the new pathway to adulthood. He wrote, "There used to be four common life phases: childhood, adolescence, adulthood and old age. Now, there are at least six: childhood, adolescence, odyssey, adulthood, active retirement and old age. Of the new ones, the least understood is odyssey, the decade of wandering that frequently occurs between adolescence and adulthood."[1] Professor Michael Kimmel, a leading researcher on men and masculinity and the author of *Guyland*, says his bird's-eye view of the dating landscape is "dizzying": "Today, I see a lot of young people leaving college and eventually they start dating and drifting in and out of a state of arrested development."[2]

Are we a generation defined by the hook-up culture of casual sexual encounters? It's true that shows like *Entourage* and *The Hills* popularize the image of singles on the prowl for a different sexual partner every night of the week. And in real life, many twenty-somethings are angsting over the protocol after a one-night stand. However, there is another storyline to Generation Y romances that sounds more like, "What should I get his mother for her birthday?" Long-term relationships are an equally common romantic state of affairs. In her "Sexplorations" column for *The Columbia Spectator*, student Miriam Datak-sokvy documented the sex lives of her peers for two-and-a-half years. She observed that there are two ways to be romantically involved when you are in college: hooking up or intense monogamy, otherwise known as the "college marriage."[3]

In fact, a Pew Research study found that about a quarter of unmarried Americans (26 percent or about 23 million adults) say they are in a committed romantic relationship[4]—this means that well over half of the eighteen- to-twenty-nine set are or are seeking to be coupled.[5]

"A Little Bit Married" is a term I coined to describe a new romantic rite of passage taking place among the urban, college-educated, under-thirty-five demographic: the long-term, unmarried relationship. Yet, despite its pervasiveness, multi-year dating for young people is terra incognita, whose terrain we are just starting to map. For Gabby, twenty-eight, the half-decade she spent dating her boyfriend was a precursor to marriage: "We had dinner with his parents, went on each other's family vacations—we basically did all the same things that we now do now that we have a marriage license." Robert, twenty-four, says A Little Bit Married is an apt description for his year-and-a-half relationship: "I realized I was in deep when I went to two Passover Seders with her, and I'm not even Jewish. We go on vacation, do holidays with each other's families, and I flew across the country for one day just to be her date at a wedding." For many, A Little Bit Married (ALBM) is a relationship pattern that they ebb in and out of for a good part of their twenties and thirties. It's not unusual, as many ALBMs noted, to stop playing house with one partner and then move in or start seriously dating another. Serial monogamy is back, except now it comes with a dog and a shared mailing address. Jason, twenty-eight, dated his girlfriend for over two years and described their dynamic as "very domesticated." "We were like an old married couple, except that we didn't have rings." Chloe, thirty-one, has been A Little Bit Married a few times in her twenties. She even went as far as talking about buying a house with one of her long-term boyfriends, stating, "You share things with the person like you are married, but you aren't, which can be quite confusing."

Signs You Are ALBM

The baseline ALBM definition I've come up with is being in a monogamous non-matrimonial relationship for at least twelve months. In practice, however, what being A Little Bit Married means varies dramatically. Maybe you and your boyfriend have lived together long enough to reach what many states would deem a legitimate common-law marriage. Or maybe you're not living together, but are fielding questions from relatives about where you two would like to eventually settle down. Perhaps you've talked about honeymoons, or made geographical adjustments to accommodate the other's career. Tara, thirty, who dated her boyfriend for four years before getting engaged, captured a prevailing theme: ALBM is all about living in the hypothetical. "When we were A Little Bit Married," she said, "everything we talked about was qualified with an 'if.' It's not the kind of conversation I would have if I were talking to my husband."

Sure, prolonged dating is full of fun coupley things: there are anniversary dinners, vacationing together, and owning a dog. But ALBM is riddled with emotional baggage. We are giving up on dream jobs and other goals to be close to our partners. We're settling for each other's foibles and imperfections as if we were married. And more often than not, we're emotionally,

QUIZ: ARE YOU A LITTLE BIT MARRIED?

1. My boyfriend and I have spent
   the last three holidays together.   YES or NO

2. We live together.   YES or NO

3. His parents and I talk on the phone.   YES or NO

4. We've been on each other's
   family vacations.   YES or NO

5. We're casual about using statements
   like, "When we get married...."   YES or NO

6. We talk about and plan for
   the future.   YES or NO

7. I often wonder, "Where is this going?"   YES or NO

8. If I got a great job in another city,
   he'd probably move for me and vice versa.   YES or NO

9. I'll be ready to get married within the
   next year.   YES or NO

10. I don't think my boyfriend is ready to
    get married anytime soon.   YES or NO

For every "Yes" give yourself a point. If you scored above a six,
you are one of the millions of ALBMs.

financially, and psychologically banking on these relationships turning into wedding invitations—when many times they don't. The consensus from those in the throes of this life stage is this: A Little Bit Married is a gray area. And a gray area is the midwife of relationship stress.

Beth, twenty-eight, says "percolating anxiety" described how she felt about the future and the meaning of the past three years that she and her boyfriend, Alex, had spent practically living together and integrating into each other's families: Where is this going? Where is the ring? Why is he not proposing if we spend every holiday with his family or mine? She explains that, "It was difficult being in a state of unknown." Beth recalls the many occasions she raised the question of her future with Alex: "At the time, he said he wanted to finish graduate school and then see where he was at. That was two years away. I was so baffled that he didn't know where we were at. I definitely felt like he was putting the brakes on the whole marriage thing. I wish I had had some guidance during that period, because it was really tough."

Nina, thirty, who has been dating her boyfriend for five years, says dating for half a decade took her by surprise: "It never occurred to me that this would be a form of a relationship . . . that I could be dating someone for this long without it being legally sanctioned by the state. Yet we definitely function like a married couple, in that we know each other's families and live together."

It's a morass of confusion out there about how to swim through this life stage toward marriage and not just tread water.

And, as Beth points out, it's hard to hold back when you get deeply entrenched with someone, not to mention their friends and family. A Little Bit Married isn't only about always having a plus-one; there are a bevy of issues with which to contend during this period of marriage-lite. Couples have to negotiate how to harmonize their career goals, how to live together and manage the problems that come with domesticating, not to mention figuring out how, or if, to take the next step—crossing the marital readiness gap. There are custody battles over the parrot or about apartments with rents that can't be paid because the "breadwinner" isn't ready to tie the knot. It's a life overshadowed by the looming questions: Is this right? If it is, how do I know? You are beyond the point of being just boyfriend and girlfriend, but you aren't married, so you exist in this constant state of limbo that even the most intrepid daters can find unsettling.

But here's the thing: Just as there are rules for casual dating, shouldn't there be rules—or at least guidelines—for relationships that will take up the better part of our early adulthood?

Why Is Everyone Dating for Such a Long Period of Time?

It's now become the norm for couples to date for three, five, even ten years.[6] But after a few years, people get restless. Lilly, twenty-six, who has been dating her boyfriend for three years and currently lives with him, says she's gotten the A Little Bit Married itch: "It's hard for me because I'm such a planner, and it feels like I have no control over when it happens." Melanie, thirty-two, now married, says she hit her wall at five years: "At our four-year anniversary, I was kind of like, whatever, but at half a decade, I thought I was wasting my life."

Many A Little Bit Marrieds say that while they've been dating, they've seen friends circle through a whole "life cycle"—they've met, gotten engaged, married, bought a house, and have had kids during the duration of the ALBM's relationship.

Here's a bit of context for why you and all your friends are plodding along with no imminent plans to send out save-the-date cards. Let's start with this: The median age for a first marriage in the United States is the highest it's ever been—27.1 for a man and 25.3 for a woman[7]—and it tips even higher in many cities. As people have postponed walking down the aisle, other new dating rituals—prolonged courtship and cohabitation—have become socially acceptable. In fact, the number of cohabiting couples has grown more than tenfold during the last forty years. Forty years ago, in 1970, only about 500,000 couples lived together in unwedded bliss; now, over five million opposite-sex couples in the United States live together outside of marriage."[8] A 2005 article in the *Detroit News* came close to calling the rise of cohabiting couples an epidemic, complete with a governmental response: "The burgeoning number of cohabiting couples—about 8 percent of American households, and most between the ages of 25 and

34—has sparked a national discussion among sociologists and researchers about the political, social and economic ramifications of so many marriage-wary people living together. It also prompted the Bush administration to push for more marriages with the Initiative for Healthy Marriage."[9] As you'll see in the chart on page 19, there is a massive cultural shift taking place about how people go about tying the knot.

A Little Bit Married is a product of modernity. We live in a time when loose and undefined dating structures have become the norm. Remember, though, that formality was a large part of the dating culture for previous generations. In early parts of the twentieth century, a man would "pin" a woman with his sports pins or give her a class ring as a sign they were now "an item." Though many have eulogized courtship and formal dating, that might be overstating and oversimplifying how people today date, but what is indisputable is that dating has fundamentally changed.

And yet, although it seems like a modern phenomenon, Dr. Helen Fisher, a Rutgers University biological anthropologist at Rutgers University and author of *Why Him? Why Her?*, says the story of A Little Bit Married is an ancient one: "Hunters and gatherers had relationships that were akin to A Little Bit Married called trial marriages. A trial marriage, very much like it is today, is when you move in and try it and see how you get along together, and if it doesn't work out, then you don't have to go through the full number of rituals. They are very common in tribal societies."[10]

DATING: THEN AND NOW

Dating	How Your Grandparents Did It	How You Do It
Age	Meet your mate, get married in your early twenties, buy a house, and have two kids by twenty-six.	Go on 875 bad dates, sign up for Match.com, and then get married in your late twenties or early thirties.
Become an adult at	Twenty-one	Thirty-five
College	Go to college to get your M.R.S. degree	Go to college to get your B.A. with high honors and then start globe-trotting.
Dating ritual	Courtship	Long-term relationship
Dating mantra	Get married	I want to find my soul mate.
Career	Work for one company and retire with a gold watch forty years later.	Work in eight different jobs before your thirtieth birthday.
Cohabitation	Living together outside of wedlock was considered scandalous.	Today, 5.2 million unmarried heterosexual couples live together.
To be married in your twenties means . . .	You were in the majority.	You are in the minority.
Conventional wisdom	You're an old maid if you're an unmarried woman at thirty.	Don't get married before you're thirty.
"Marriage is forever"	What people believed.	What? I was raised by a single parent.

Fast forward a few thousand years to the 1850s and you can also see the origins of A Little Bit Married, according to Kathleen Gerson, a sociology professor at New York University. She argues that, as the industrial revolution proceeded, adult children were gradually freed from parental control over their choice of when and whom to marry. Men and women became increasingly free to choose their mates, and romantic love, based on a couple's sense of compatibility and shared feelings, became the ideal.[11] A Little Bit Married is that idea on steroids: It's the ultimate statement that taking your wedding vows is a genuine choice.

Jeffrey Arnett, a research professor who studies twenty-somethings and the author of a seminal book on young adults called *Emerging Adults*, attributes the radical change in courtship to the loosening up on the timeline of when someone should become an adult. "The concept of emerging adults," he states, "didn't even exist before Gen Ys, because in previous generations there was no transition into adulthood, you just become one." Today, there's a common conversation between parents and children that often sounds something along the lines of: "When I was your age, I already had a mortgage, a career-track job, and your mom was pregnant with your little brother." The zeitgeist today, however, is captured by lines like: "I'm in no rush. There are developing countries to visit and graduate degrees to be accrued." The timeline to adulthood now looks a lot like the continent of Africa—sprawling.

Arnett's analysis mirrors what the vast majority of the men and women I interviewed expressed: What's the hurry? Right, exactly, especially when there are multiple careers to be forged and climates to be cooled. Mark Golin, the former editor of the lad magazine *Maxim*, described how an American man's adolescence may now last until age thirty-five or forty: "In the past you grew up at 21 and you were a sober, productive part of society. Now, you have guys who are 35-year-old 17-year-olds. When it comes to dating, they're out pulling some girl's pigtails. It is not grown-up behavior."[12]

Flexibility Is Convenient

Another factor driving us toward long-term dating is the scattered geography that fosters a great deal of impermanence. Young people today lead a peripatetic lifestyle. The map of a twenty-something life often looks like a cross-country road trip or an around-the-world ticket. You grew up in Denver, went to college in Boston, migrated to New York for your first job, did a stint abroad in Australia, and then moved to Washington, D.C., for your second job. Nathan, twenty-five, is one of these nomads. From college in San Francisco to a year abroad in Chile to his first job in New York, he is now on the brink of transplanting himself again, this time to graduate school, which could mean going back to San Francisco or perhaps to Boston or Philadelphia. He has been dating his girlfriend Allison for three years, but says ring shopping is not on his to-do list. "I still want flexibility," he says. "I want to go to business school and figure out what I want my career to be. I still want to travel with friends."

Barbara Dafoe Whitehead, the co-director of The National Marriage Project at Rutgers University, wrote, "Neither men nor women have the time or a pressing desire for marriage, especially when they can get some marriage-like benefits without it. So they put it off and enter into relationships that offer some combination of sex, companionship, convenience, and economies of scale."[13] But even economies of scale have issues. How are these career calculations impacting long-term relationships? Is career first and love second in the calculus for both men and women? These are questions that Chapter 3—"Career Compromises and Christmas Trees: Should You Be Acting Married When You Aren't?"—will tackle.

Perhaps, though, the most widely touted reason for today's new dating landscape is a tiny little pill. The birth control pill (and easily accessible contraception in general) changed the face of courtship irrevocably by eliminating sex as the main impetus for marriage. Men and women could now have sex with less fear of committing to childrearing responsibilities. Today, premarital sex is the norm, with the exception of small pockets within religious communities. Birth control ranks up there with the vote as an agent of female liberation. It's given generations of women control of their fertility and marriage timetables and allowed them to wield their sexual freedom in ways that has made it possible for them to forge careers and marry for love. In the process, the birth control pill has produced its own offspring: A Little Bit Married. As Mike, twenty-eight, who is in a long-term relationship, puts it: "If I had to be married to have sex, I would probably be married, as would every guy I know."

Looking for Mr. (and Ms.) Perfect

What does this all mean for the millions of us trying to figure out how, when, or if to get married? It seems that we are now mining our relationships for intangibles. Rather than marrying for sex and money, the twenty-first-century relationship is based more on abstractions, like love and compatibility— giving way to some Mt. Everest–sized expectations. Adam, twenty-eight, when trying to explain the reason he broke it off with his girlfriend of five years, said, "I don't know, I just stopped getting those butterflies in my stomach every time I saw her." However, Adam could have been any number of people interviewed for this book. The stakes for coupling have never been higher. Contentment has become ever more elusive as marriage has gone from an economic to a romantic contract. It has prolonged the time we spend looking at our current partner for signs of a soul mate.

Keep in mind that the soul mate is a rather novel concept in our romantic history. Marriage used to be much more utilitarian. Love was a factor, but that's not why couples ended up at the altar: Women needed a base of economic support, and sex outside of marriage was considered too risky before the advent of birth control. Esther Perel, a marriage and family therapist and the author of *Mating in Captivity*, says what we now expect from one person is what a community used to provide: "We are looking for the staples of marriage—economic stability and family—plus some. So it's not that one thing has replaced another. It's the addition of all these other things."[14] But who could blame us for wanting this magic—and some might argue unattainable—mix of qualities in our partners? As our life spans increase, you could easily be celebrating forty-five-, fifty-, or sixty-year wedding anniversaries. The notion that we could spend five or six decades with one person has given new weight to the words "I do."

And marriage can be an even more daunting prospect for a generation that spent their weekends being shuttled between two different houses and could say "joint custody" before they were even out of diapers. Jonah, twenty-six, witnessed his parents endure an extremely acrimonious divorce. "It's made me scared about getting married. I just want to be sure," is how he explains why he ended his two-year relationship with his girlfriend. "I just didn't have that certainty, but I think that's because I was so scarred by the model of my parents' marriage."

Of course, being A Little Bit Married isn't fueled only by growing up in non-nuclear families, commitment phobia, or the wish to write a smaller rent check every month. For many— even those that came from nuclear families—marriage can look like a treacherous institution that should come prepackaged with a full-body, steel armor suit and a helmet. Allison, twenty-eight, who was in a relationship for two years before she got engaged, summed up a common sentiment about the romantic rite of passage and the feeling of wanting to enter marriage well equipped and well informed: "It's given me a big window of time to see how he interacts with my family and friends and feel more confident about taking the next step."

THE SIX SIGNS OF MODERN DATING

1. Cohabitation is the norm.
It's not living in sin, it's just living like the rest of your friends.

2. Hooking up isn't our only romantic ambition.
A term as popular as the *booty text* is the *college marriage*.

3. We hold off on ring shopping.
This generation has been told to take their time. The twenties are one's odyssey years of exploring and experimenting.

4. We aren't going to settle.
An overwhelming majority (94%) of never-married singles between 20–29 agree that "when you marry you want your spouse to be your soul mate, first and foremost."[15]

5. She is (still) ready before he is.
A 2005 poll on Gen Ys found that women were a bit more eager: 55 percent wanted to get married in the next five years, compared to 42 percent of men[16].

6. "Men bring home the bacon" and "women raise the children" is a thing of the past.
Today, Gen Ys are placing more value on forging egalitarian relationships. The notion that "a man is a financial plan" is an anachronism.

What You Will Find Inside

Here's a brief geography of this book:

- What are the main markers of marriage without marriage?
- What does it mean to date in a time when we have another decade before we have to "grow up"?
- How do issues about careers, living together, and religion get figured out when there isn't a ring?
- Why—and in what ways—is this romantic rite of passage different for men than for women?

To that last question, Chapters 5 and 6—"The Female Proposal" and "I Do. Or Do I?"—probe more about the gender dynamics of A Little Bit Married, but it's such a pervasive undercurrent of this relationship stage that I want to wave at it early on. Yes, we've seen a woman run for president, vice president, and, in general, women are breaking all types of glass ceilings. Yet there is still a relationship ceiling where many women hit their heads. The source? There's a fundamental power imbalance when it comes to the decision of when to get married. In the vast majority of cases, it's still the man who sets the marriage timeline, leaving many women wondering and waiting about the future of their relationship. Brynn, twenty-six, like many A Little Bit Marrieds, said there was no mutual timeline: "Even though Jack and I had been dating for five years, it was his timeline and it was assumed he would propose when he was ready. I felt like I was marching to the beat of his drum." Brynn and many other women hit on a passivity that is endemic to A Little Bit Married. The common echo from women in the stage of "waiting to seal the deal" was that being A Little Bit Married can feel like running an emotional marathon, except you aren't always sure whether there is a finish line.

Interviews with former and current A Little Bit Marrieds are the backbone of this book. The real-life stories, insights, and advice have shaped the topics explored in the next seven chapters. In those coming chapters, you'll be hearing from a slew of experts ranging from psychologists to sociologists to anthropologists to relationship experts. Melding my own reporting with the texture of expert advice and opinions, *A Little Bit Married* will help you sort out the following:

- How to read the signs about whether or not you're headed to the altar
- How to have those tough conversations in which you address the big questions: Where is this going? How can we reconcile our religious and political differences? What are our views about money? Do we both have the same vision for the future?
- How much you should be acting married if you aren't
- What to do if you or your partner is unsure about whether the other person is "the one"

- Whether moving in together is a good idea
- How to move on after a long-term relationship ends
- How to take the step from A Little Bit Married
  to Married

This generation is in the process of writing its relationship history. Historians, anthropologists, and sociologists will look back and document that Gen Ys took part in a series of long-term relationships before saying "I do." A Little Bit Married is defined by more than sharing a mailing address, splitting the bills, or having joint custody over Fido. More than those physical markers, it's defined by the length of time of that the relationship lasts. The sprint to the aisle is a gait of another generation. We now seek less corporeal elements in a partner, and instead we are after something more squishy and hard to pin down—love, compatibility, and friendship—and, in doing so, heralding new types of commitment structures.

What follows is an excavation of this new romantic rite of passage. The following chapters will peel through the various layers, discuss the practical realities, and be peppered it with both real-life stories and expert advice. On that note, let's start with a topic that frames a central part of the A Little Bit Married conversation: the new trails to adulthood.

A Little Bit Married Rules

As I conducted my 120th ALBM interview, common themes and threads began to emerge. So at the end of each chapter, you'll find a few A Little Bit Married "Rules"—2.0 style. The following quartet are some general principles. At the end of each of the following chapters, you'll find more specific ones.

Be Honest with Yourself

Will you be happy if the status quo remains the same for the next two years without any commitment about the future? Do you even want to get married? Do you want to have children? Do some soul-searching about what you want from the relationship. That way, you'll be able to have an honest and empowered conversation with your partner about how, when, or if, to take the next step.

Ask the Right Questions

Yes, you can berate your partner with the vague four-word question: Where is this going? However, that might not help you get your finger on the pulse of what you really what to know. Take a more specific route and pose questions about career goals, priorities in life, and where does s/he see himself at thirty-five.

Set Time Frames

This one is geared toward the ladies. Time is the most valued commodity of the twenty-first century. Yet there's an epidemic of women out there who waste precious years of their lives, hoping that hope will proffer a marriage proposal. The consensus regarding this was that you should be firm about how long you'll tolerate the inertia.

Don't Make Assumptions

Emma, twenty-nine, assumed that Ted, her boyfriend of three and a half years, would factor her into his decision about where to move after graduate school. She stated that, "I was floored when he said to me, 'I think we should both just take the best job we are offered.'" Emma assumed that the three years they spent having a long-distance relationship between London and New York, countless weekends spent with the other person's family, and simply the duration of the relationship created an iron-clad contract that, after two years of long distance, they would try to end up in the same time zone. Find out if you are the same page (i.e. ask questions such as: Are we are on the same page about taking jobs in the same city after business school?).

2
Dating
Peter Pan

———— ❧ ————

You're Ready to Register
at Pottery Barn and
He's Playing Grand Theft Auto

> Everywhere I turn today I see men who
> refuse to grow up—husbands of thirty-five who are
> enjoying playing the same video games that obsess
> twelve-year-olds; boyfriends who will not commit
> to marriage or family.
>
> —Gary Cross, author of *Men to Boys*

In a review of the 2006 Zach Braff movie *The Last Kiss*, the *New York Sun* described the theme as "the crisis of coming of age." But this wasn't a film about turning eighteen, twenty-one, or even twenty-five. *The Last Kiss* is a movie about turning thirty.[1] Two years after the release of *The Last Kiss*, Kay Hymowitz, a Senior Fellow at the Manhattan Institute, a policy research think tank, and a contributing editor of *City Journal*, coined the phrase "child-man" in order to describe the phenomenon of many young men lingering

(happily) in a new hybrid state between semi-hormonal adolescence and responsible self-reliance: "He lives with his single guy friends, goes out to bars where he picks up a wide
variety of women, and sees an afternoon of playing Halo or
basketball with a few of his buddies as the ideal way to spend
a decade,"[2] Hymowitz wrote. That's just the tip of the Peter
Pan iceberg.

Forget endless nights spent playing Guitar Hero or the con-
viction that "buddy night" is sacrosanct. Those are manageable
compared to the glacial pace at which many child-men move
their relationships. Just ask Maya, twenty-seven, who has been
dating her boyfriend for eight years: "John wants to be in a
committed relationship, but he says being married is for when
he is old. He just turned twenty-eight and still thinks he is a
kid, while I have a career-tracked job and am ready to take
things to the next level." In a similar situation, Rebecca,
twenty-seven, says the guy she dated for five years—through
college and law school—was more interested in continuing
the frat party than in making any kind of commitment to her
or investing seriously in their relationship. She states that,
"The partying, drinking, and the constant hankering to be with
'his guys' was a big strain on our relationship. There wasn't
really any room for me. I was always wondering when he
would outgrow it, but he didn't seem to have any interest in
adulthood."

Drew, twenty-eight, lives with his girlfriend of four years
and says she is a few steps ahead of him on the marriage
timetable. He readily attributes it to his Peter Pan phase—a

lifestyle where alcohol and male bonding still reign supreme. His priorities are: bromance then romance. He shares: "I think the drinking and constantly hanging out with my guy friends is a problem in our relationship, but I'm not quite ready to give that up." What emerges here is that men, understandably, want to enjoy their "youth" and have some version of commitment without commitment—to have the freedom to go out and "do what they want," as many men explained it. What Drew describes, however, is a window into a rather insidious side of the child-man. Like many men his age, Drew wants the comforts and accoutrements of a relationship without having to make the full load of sacrifices. The more charitable viewpoint here is that adulthood—and, by proxy, marriage—doesn't always jive with working entry-level jobs and sharing a bathroom with four roommates, which is the reality for many A Little Bit Marrieds. Evan, twenty-nine, who has been dating his girlfriend for over six years, says that he still feels "like a child" because his job as a freelancer is so erratic that he never knows where his next paycheck is coming from, or if it's coming. He goes on to say that, "It's hard to think of yourself as an adult when you don't have a full-time, nine-to-five office job, are barely making enough money to cover your own expenses, and still have roommates. I take solace in the fact that you don't see sixty-year-olds crumpled up and dying, so you feel like you have a lot more time to hit those markers."

The child-man signs, however, don't tell the whole story. In many cases, playing Grand Theft Auto ad nauseum and living in some version of Sigma Chi–turns-twenty-eight doesn't give

EIGHT SIGNS THAT YOU ARE
DATING A CHILD-MAN

1. He constantly tells you he doesn't feel like a grown-up and doesn't seem interested in achieving the milestones of adulthood (i.e., career-tracked job, commitment, financial security) anytime soon.

2. He's in his late twenties and has never dated anyone for longer than three months.

3. He shuts down when you want to talk about the future or, for that matter, any difficult emotional conversation.

4. He doesn't know what he wants to do with his life and is taking few steps to figure it out.

5. He rarely compromises or sacrifices anything for you. In general, his character in a movie would be cast at the "feckless" type.

6. His mom still does his laundry (or other signs he's not quite emancipated from his family).

7. You fall somewhere after video games, drinking, and football on his list of priorities.

8. He believes commitment is compatible with turning forty.

the full picture of the prolonged adolescence. So what else should you be paying attention to in order to glean insight into whether the guy you are dating will ever leave Never Never Land? First, look at what kind of compromises he is willing make for the relationship. Is he generous with his time and energy? Does he seem ready and excited about factoring a long-term girlfriend into his next life-phase? The child-man psychology has an aura of impermanence, but not just in a sense that he's a flight risk. Rather, it's a quality that manifests as a reticence to solidify any future plans. This certainly is the case for Robert, twenty-five, a mild-mannered guy who has been dating his girlfriend, Caroline, for over two years. He is applying to graduate schools all over the country, but is adamant that he doesn't want company. Robert, like many young people, is employing the calculus of career first, relationship second, but also reflects a staple of immaturity called, "I haven't really thought about that." His philosophy about the relationship is: "I'm just taking it week to week."

Being A Little Bit Married can obfuscate the real temperature of the relationship. In other words, although people can be acting in a way that signals a long-term commitment, it is dangerous to assume that just because you eat dinner together five nights a week and have met his family you are within arm's length, particularly when it comes to men in this transient life-phase. The only way to get to the other side of the muddled and murky odyssey years is to take a thermometer to the relationship. We'll get to more on how to do that shortly.

Another iteration of the man-child is the guy who, after three years of dating while edging on thirty, is still aimless about the direction of the relationship. Beth, twenty-eight, is now married to Alex. They dated for almost three years before he proposed and, during those thirty-six months, Beth says there were many moments she felt "extremely frustrated" by what she perceived as his dawdling: "We were spending almost every night together, going on each other's family vacations and, it seemed to me, deeply intertwining our lives, but Alex just wasn't ready to get married. He kept saying he needed more time."

However, Alex's "dillydallying" about getting down on one knee wasn't about his need to spend more time mastering his beer pong game. Instead, it was about financial security and establishing himself professionally. This is an important distinction. Although there are many man-children out there who embody the archetype of the commitment-phobic man, there's also another dynamic at play. The new order of adulthood typical of this generation is to establish yourself in your career before getting married. And these aren't our parents' careers we are trying to forge—going to work for one company and retiring forty years later with a gold watch is a vestige of the past. Today, finding a career is an exceedingly long and demanding process that involves, at the least, a graduate degree, probably a few rounds of trial and error, and multiple relocations.

Although women are hardly impervious to these labor-market forces, their career choices and professions don't correlate as directly to their marital ambitions as they do for men. Research has consistently shown that whether and when a man marries is closely tied to the adequacy and stability of his earnings.[3]

Why Are Women Seemingly Ready for Marriage Sooner?

The grating voice in all of us could say, "Well, if he really loved me, then he'd propose, despite thousands of dollars in student loans, no steady source of income, or the fact that he is in the middle of a grueling residency where he sleeps twenty hours a week." You think to yourself, "I'm not sure where I'm going in my career, I have debt to pay off, or I'm about to start law school, and that's not standing between me and a Vera Wang dress." Right, of course, that's because young men and women often have different sets of priorities and don't travel the same road to adulthood. Not only are the priorities dissimilar, but the cultural messages for men and women surrounding marriage play very different soundtracks. Many have pointed to the double standard of bachelor vs. spinster in order to spotlight how society sends different signals to men and women about marriage. For men, the message is that life without a wife is liberation, and for women it's a hex and a condition that must be overcome at any and all costs. The reality check is that men do want get married, but there is just an added layer of social pressure for women. As Meghan O'Rourke, *Slate's* culture critic, astutely observed on this topic, "Women still measure their worth in relationship to marriage in ways that men don't."[4]

"In general, for women, they look forward to growing up and the milestones that come with that—family, career, and independence—and guys kind of dread it," says Michael Kimmel, author of *Guyland*. "Men, on the other hand," he observes, "view adulthood as the negation of boyhood, a period in your life where you get to piss on bonfires and fart and not have to apologize for it. They look at adulthood as having to wear a tie and take orders from a boss who knows less than you." But the expectations surrounding adulthood are there for women, too. Diana, twenty-nine, who is now married, says she subscribed to the idea that "we are all supposed to think that we are already adults by the time you get married, as opposed to this is a person that I want to grow into adulthood with."

Although the terms "child-man" and "Peter Pan" might sound pejorative, a prolonged adolescence is simply a sign of the times, in some ways, for both men and women. Now that people's life expectancies are so much longer, careers are something of which you have seven or eight, and it's socially acceptable to get married well after thirty—the twenties now read as a decade of practice or free time. Peter—and, to be fair, Paula—Pans are products of the late twentieth and early twenty-first centuries, says Stephanie Coontz, a professor of history and family studies at The Evergreen State College and author of *Marriage, a History*, an erudite overview of the institution. She states that, "It used to be that marriage was the way you embarked upon adulthood. Today, it's the culmination of adulthood. It's what you do when you've established yourself financially and emotionally. More and more, it's about two already formed people coming together."[5]

A common echo from men is: "I have another decade of my life before I have to grow up," says Jason, twenty-five. After comparing his life to his father's, who was settled down and married in his twenties, Jason doesn't see his twenties arcing the same way for him: "Marriage is for the future, like when I'm thirty, so I can have kids by thirty-three or thirty-four. I think I have to be at a certain point in my career and financially secure. I don't want to look back when I'm married and feel like I had any regrets about not doing things in my twenties." And this isn't necessarily such a bad thing for either sex. As Kimmel argues, "The advancing age of marriage, for example, benefits both women and men, who have more time to explore career opportunities, not to mention establishing their identities, before committing to home and family."[6]

But shelving all the valid cultural and historical reasons why the man-child has turned into an icon that pops up in every Judd Apatow movie, it's also a life stage that wreaks havoc on hoards of long-term relationships.

What Makes a Guy Ready to Grow Up?

In the Disney version of Peter Pan, Peter remains in Never Never Land, passing up his opportunity to marry Wendy. Back on planet earth, most men aren't passing up the opportunity to marry "Wendy." The vast majority of men do not decide to permanently relocate to Never Never Land, but they do have fears and hesitations about the foray into adulthood and marriage. Aaron, twenty-nine, who is now engaged to his girlfriend of seven years, says that he felt a lot of pressure to be "a man" before he proposed. Describing what those expectations felt like, he explains, "There was a huge financial component for me. I had to figure out where I was going before I dragged someone else along with me." The sentiment that Aaron and many other young men express is that although they fully expect their wives to work and bring home some of the proverbial bacon, they still feel pressure to be the breadwinner or put themselves on a career-track where they'll have the resources to support a family.

Dr. Scott Stanley, a research professor of psychology and codirector of the Center for Marital and Family Studies at the University of Denver, addressed this issue in a paper entitled, "What Is It with Men and Commitment, Anyway?" at the Sixth Annual Smart Marriages conference. The crux of his theory is that men see the line between "marriage" and "not-marriage" differently than women do. In other words, for women the marital readiness factor isn't as entangled in what their tax returns looked like that year. To that point, Stanley found that men's fears about commitment tend to concern some very tangible bread-and butter-issues—namely, that there will be some financial loss incurred by marriage (even though research shows that men's incomes increase when they get married[7]) and that women will want to have children sooner than they will. Men see popping the question as involving a distinct set of life changes that they would like to defer for as long as possible because it means leaving their carefree days behind them and taking on a role—husband—that comes with some daunting financial expectations. As Stanley put it,

> [Men] associate marriage with the expectancy of having to grow up. That step across the line will have a powerful impact on their lives. If they can, many men will resist this until quite late into their 20s, because marriage seems to have a big effect on how men think about themselves, what they do, what a woman can ask of them, and what they're willing to give. This may be the very reason why men are widely seen as resisting getting married, especially in comparison to women. They believe that crossing the line has many implications for how they have to behave and what they need to give to their female partners. There are surely many exceptions, but I think, on average, it's different for women.[8]

Fun and Freedom First

The Mecca of marriage research, the National Marriage Project at Rutgers University, a pro-marriage research and analysis institution that studies the state of marriage in the United States, conducted a study in 2004 called "Which Men Marry and Why" that empirically confirmed the reasons many of the men interviewed for this book cite about dragging their feet toward marriage. The study, which was a nationally representative sample of men aged twenty-five to thirty-four, found that 53 percent of the unmarried men in the sample agree that they are "not interested in getting married any time soon." Three-quarters of those men agree with the statement "at this stage in my life I want fun and freedom."

In addition to "fun and freedom," these men cite a number of other reasons for putting off marriage, including the challenges of the marital search itself; the time constraints on dating imposed by work obligations; and the need to achieve financial viability, or the proxies of financial viability, such as a house or nice wedding.[9]

Job and Financial Security

Aaron, twenty-nine, says his hesitation about proposing had little to do with doubts about making a long-term commitment to his then-girlfriend: "I wanted to marry her, but I was in graduate school and didn't really have a job. My take was, 'Let me get through school first and then we can talk about getting married.' I know the hold-up for some guys is fear and commitment phobia, but I think the equally common hold-up for men is that they want to feel like an established person in the world before they propose." Jason, twenty-eight, says his undefined career path is the biggest obstacle standing between him and proposing to his girlfriend of four years: "It's not that I don't want to marry my girlfriend—I'm not old enough and don't think I'm well enough established to support a family. How could I have a kid in a one-bedroom apartment?" Drew, also twenty-eight, lives with his girlfriend and they have been dating for four years. Asked about what he's waiting for, he says his hesitancy is—guess what—career-related! "At twenty-eight, I'm just not where I thought I would be. I mean, I like my job. But I'd like a better title."

Timing

These findings should be taken in concert with another critical bit of data: The majority of men do want to get married, surprisingly even more than women do, according to national polling.[10] The rub here is the time frame. The challenge for couples is figuring out when to walk down the aisle. According to Kimmel, the data points in marriage's favor: "Married men are the ones who have the most sex, lowest smoking rates, and lowest levels of depression. Men, for the most part, seem to be aware that marriage vastly improves their quality of life. Virtually every guy I spoke with said he wanted to get married someday, and that he hoped he would be happy," says Kimmel.[11]

Take Marnie and Tim as an example of a couple who mastered this timing challenge. Around their fifth ALBM anniversary, Marnie's marriage light blazed on, something she expressed repeatedly to Tim. But Tim had just moved across the country for her, leaving a lucrative job in the wake, and was attempting to get his financial bearings in a new city. "Like so many women," Marnie relates, "I wanted him to be dying to marry me. When we talked about getting married, Tim would say that we didn't have any money and he wanted to wait until he re-established himself." The epilogue to this story is that Tim did propose to Marnie—not as soon as she would have liked, but, as she says now, "Women are often just a little bit ahead of guys on the timing of everything, from when to propose to making the bed." The sooner you can accept that, the happier you'll be, say the masses of A Little Bit Marrieds.

So What Can You Do?

But now what? Yes, it's comforting to know that your boyfriend isn't some lone unicorn lingering alone in this weird wasteland of semi-adulthood—in fact, there's an epidemic of relationships just like yours—but what do you do while he's still Peter Panning and you're ready to start your adult life?

Define the Relationship

If being A Little Bit Married were to have a tagline it would be: "Knowing is always better than not." Pushing for clarity is critical for couples who are A Little Bit Married. Stanley says one of the salient take-aways from his research is that women should be having the "DTR"—Define The Relationship talk— sooner rather than later. Yet this doesn't happen at the rate it probably should. Why? Perhaps for the same reasons that women don't negotiate for salaries: the fear factor that someone could say no or they'll be perceived as pushy or aggressive. These reasons explain, at least in part, why women are tepid about having the DTR. On the salary front, women stand to lose hundreds of thousands of dollars over the course of their lifetime by not negotiating, and though the effects of not having a DTR aren't as monetarily quantifiable, women do lose something valuable—time.

How to Have the DTR

Get a sense of his priorities. A useful image here is Maslow's hierarchy—that famous pyramid that ranks human needs. Think of the DTR as finding out what his personal pyramid looks like. Is it job at the top and relationship at the bottom? Or vice versa? Before you dive right in and ask, "So where do I factor into your life plans?"—which could catch someone a little off guard—frame it in more open-ended terms, such as, "So what factors are you considering when deciding whether to take the job in San Francisco or the one in Chicago?" If he doesn't list you, then ask, "Where do I factor in?"

Don't fall into the "you don't love me" trap. Rachel, thirty, says when she and her long-term boyfriend were in the awkward limbo stage of trying to figure out whether or not to take the next step, she used to equate any deviation from the relationship script she had written in her head with "he doesn't love me." The reality is that it's rare to be completely in sync on the timing of a relationship. Remember that being A Little Bit Married has very little in common with synchronized swimming.

Be direct.   Diana, twenty-nine, approached hints of a lingering adolescence with her long-term boyfriend, who she is now married to, by being very clear about what she was looking for: "I told him that I wasn't interested in thirty-three-year-old men who aren't grown up, and that if he really felt like he wasn't an adult yet or ready to entertain the possibility of marriage, then this was not the relationship for him."

Make the distinction.   Neil Chethik, author of *VoiceMale* and the first syndicated columnist on men's lives, says it boils down to making the critical distinction between two types of men: men who aren't ready to get married and men who aren't ready to get married right now. "My advice is to separate what you need and want from what the man needs and wants. If you want to get married and he's not ready, I think you should ask yourself how long are you willing to wait for him to be ready?"[12]

All cultural signs seem to indicate that the Peter Pan boyfriend is here to stay. In fact, it wouldn't be surprising if in ten years "emerging adulthood" nests itself in the developmental lexicon the same way "adolescence" has. What can change, however, is how couples navigate the transition to adulthood. Understanding what marriage means to men, the roots of their

> ## THREE SURVIVAL TIPS FOR DATING A CHILD-MAN
>
> **1.** Take your life seriously and act like an adult even if he won't.
>
> **2.** Read the handwriting on the wall. What do his choices and actions say about his desire and commitment to become an adult who is ready to get married?
>
> **3.** Communicate about how you both view this stage in your lives in order to determine whether there is any overlap between your time frames for growing up.

fears and hesitations, and how this impacts their identity is critical for any woman in a long-term relationship. Gaining a firmer grasp of what saying, "Till death do us part" means emotionally, psychologically, and financially for that guy with whom you are playing house is more than just helpful context; it's the way to avoid the typical and recycled conversation lines between the sexes—such as Why won't you commit? Why are you pressuring me to grow up? Where is the ring?—that usually just culminate in finger-pointing, blaming, resentment, and the perpetuation of glib notions that men are from Mars and women are from Venus. To that point, marriage scholars like Coontz agree that this knee-jerk reaction of "men are afraid of commitment" needs to be muted because it's a fiction: "More men than women say marriage is an ideal lifestyle. But they don't always seem to be able to translate that abstraction into a set of behaviors that leads them to marriage," says Coontz. Professor Gary Cross, author of *Men to Boys*, sees the obstacle to dialogue in terms of the binary model men are given between the strong and silent type or being completely emasculated: "You're either Judge Hardy or Steve Martin in Cheaper by the Dozen. The choice between the old patriarch and the boy-man is not viable. We need to start thinking about more of a middle ground."[13]

The middle ground, however, should not be a place for men to opt out of a commitment. Rather, it's a place for ALBMs to start talking about adulthood and marriage, a conversation that men should be equally interested in having and starting. After all, marriage certainly comes with just as many—if not more—sweeteners for men as it is does for women.

Admittedly, asking your boyfriend, "So . . . how do you feel about adulthood and what do you see as its main markers and where are you time-wise on meeting them?" doesn't quite roll off the tongue easily. Just as "Could you make me an Excel spreadsheet with your timeline mapped out and some Outlook meeting planners when you might be ready to grow up?" certainly doesn't fall into the pillow-talk category. Yes, it can seem like a clumsy conversation topic, but there are ways to have it gracefully. Here are some conversation starters:

- Do you feel pressure to be in a certain financial position before you get married?
- What's your view of marriage? Is it two fully formed, financially independent people coming together, or do you see a model where a couple forms and grows together?
- When you think about your life, do you have set goals you want to meet by a certain age? Or do you just take it as it comes?

A Little Bit Married Rules

Keep in mind that men and women in the A Little Bit Married demographic take different pathways to adulthood. Despite all of the advances women have made, the marital-readiness factor is less tied to their earning potential. Although as women increasingly make strides in the workplace this is certainly changing, it's still not as direct of a marriage predictor as it is for men. Conversely, men see marriage as signing into an institution that not only says "Till death to us part," but is also a declaration of "I must provide."

If sixty is the new forty, then thirty practically makes you a zygote. It's the dawning of the age of the man-child, a generation of men who aren't in any hurry to reach the milestones—house, wife, and kids—that once marked adulthood. Instead, they are taking their time to get down on one knee, a dynamic that leaves many A Little Bit Married couples at odds about their marriage timetables. Although Paula Pans do exist, they aren't quite as ubiquitous as Peters, lending credence to psychological theories and research that show that becoming "an adult" has different landmarks for men than women. For men, marriage is deeply entrenched in (perhaps) outdated notions about breadwinning. Alas, modernity has not yet caught up with male psychology. Researchers point out that crossing the line to marriage is a step that has a lot do to with the proverbial bread and butter: The pre-proposal process puts the question—"Will I be able to provide?"—flashing on their radar screen. Women, however, don't factor income or their life-long earning potential into their marriage timetable to quite the same degree. And there you have the perfect-storm conditions for relationship tension. The bright spot is that this is a passing life stage and that couples can—and do—find ways to grow up together.

3
Career Compromises and Christmas Trees

———— ❖ ————

Should You Be Acting Married
When You Aren't?

Haven't you wondered why so many people overlook issues and differences in their dating relationships only to have these problems plague their marriages years later? You are dumbfounded when your friend forgives her boyfriend (or his girlfriend) for that destructive and repeating pattern of behavior that everyone else can see ... but then it happens to you.

—John Van Epp, *How to Avoid Marrying a Jerk*

Maya, twenty-seven, has had, by anyone's account, an epic relationship. She and her boyfriend, Brian, have been dating for almost a decade. They met in college, became fast friends, and, after the first semester, decided that they were soul mates. "We were the most unlikely pair," Maya says, referring to their diverse backgrounds. Maya is African American and from a small town in the south, and Brian is Jewish and was raised in New York City. Religion has been a sticking point: "As Brian gets older, he's become more adamant about raising his kids Jewish, which means I would have to convert, something that I'm not sure I want to do."

Though it's definitely advisable to sort out whether you want a Christmas tree, a Chanukah bush, or a menorah and a Santa Claus before you get married, these marriage-esque issues are staples of the A Little Bit Married lifestyle. There is bargaining about everything from finances to friendships to family to food. Maya has weathered it all. On the career front, she says, "I made the decision to move from Los Angeles where I had a great life—an upwardly mobile job, an active social life, and sunny weather year-round—to New York. After I moved, my quality of life declined significantly. I kept asking myself, 'What have I gotten myself into?'"

By definition, A Little Bit Married is a test stage, which means it's chock-full of different types of experiments, whether that means moving to Beijing when the only Chinese you know is "ni hao" or giving up your penchant for hamburgers because your girlfriend is a strict vegetarian. There is certainly a compelling argument to be made for making sacrifices and accommodations. In fact, "relationship" and "compromise" are practically interchangeable terms. As for the experimentation that goes on during the ALBM years, you certainly can't live in a sanitized relationship test tube where no one ever takes risks or puts themselves on the line. A Little Bit Marrieds make these sacrifices because they want to stretch the bandwidth of the relationship and test drive whether they want to continue making those sacrifices and compromises for the rest of their lives. And a lot times it works out well to take a pay cut or move a bit off the geographic radar as part of the A Little Bit Married experiment. Remember that Hillary Clinton followed Bill to Arkansas, hardly the epicenter of career opportunities for a Yale Law School graduate.

Although everything more or less worked out for Hillary, the other side of the coin is that these sacrifices are made from a place of overvaluing the relationship, which leaves some tough questions unanswered and unhappy living arrangements in sleepy towns. The goal of this chapter is not to sound the alarm bells that you should expunge all of the spontaneity from your relationship or drive a hard line that you must be married if you are going to make the kind of sacrifices that married people typically make. Rather, its purpose is to raise the question of how exuberant people in this relationship stage should be when it comes to making life-shaping and -changing decisions based on the other person? This chapter will look at the practical and psychological elements of this part of the A Little Bit Married experience. Specifically, what regrets do people have when they sacrifice in a long-term relationship? What issues should you consider before you sacrifice for someone to whom you are not married? Do men and women view sacrifice and compromise differently? How can you find out if you both are on the same page about what making this accommodation means for the relationship?

On the cautionary-tale front, Nitten, twenty-eight, started making some rather steep sacrifices for his live-in girlfriend.

He shares that, "I had enough money saved to keep me going for a year while I worked on my screenplay. My girlfriend, though, kept losing her job, and I ended up supporting us on my rainy day savings. I got very resentful."

Chloe, thirty-one, says she serially put her life and career plans on hold to help a long-term boyfriend, stating that, "I was always helping out my partner. I'd work an extra job so he could go and do what he needed."

Maya says her decision is tainted with a very palpable sense of regret. She left what she described as a "fabulous job" in Los Angeles to move to a city that she wasn't crazy about to be with her unemployed boyfriend who, as she found out after she'd signed a lease and unpacked, wasn't ready to commit to her. And Nitten says the resentment toward his girlfriend about supporting her financially became so unbearable that it completely destroyed the relationship. Chloe, who is now engaged, also said that the constant compromising stagnated her career.

His and Her Compromises

It's not hard to imagine that after two, three, or four years of dating someone, you could find yourself in at least one situation that required you to think about how—or if—you wanted to factor that person into either your immediate or long-term future. Couple that with the nomadic patterns of this generation, and the "Should I move for him/her?" is the most frequently had ALBM conversation. However, there's a "his" and a "her" storyline here. When it comes to making sacrifices in a relationship, research by Dr. Sarah Whitton, a psychologist and researcher at Boston University, found that men and women view it differently. "The gender differences are the big story here," she says about the research she's done on this topic. Whitton explains that, "The main thing our study shows is that women tend to act like they are married—making sacrifices like spending Christmas with their boyfriend's family and moving across the country for someone who may not yet have fully committed to them. The research indicates that women might be making a lot of these big sacrifices thinking that it means the relationship is headed toward marriage." Putting her findings in broader gender terms, Whitton says, "Men need to see a clear future together in order to sacrifice for their partner, whereas women tend to base these big decisions about sacrifice on more subjective feelings of love and attachment. We know from basic psychology research that people attribute the same motivation to others that we have for ourselves."[1] Translation: You are taking religious conversion classes because you believe you two are in it for the long haul and assume, because you think that, so does he. But what Whitton's research found is that that might not be the case. Still, the common thread, for both men and women, is that the issue usually surfaces around careers and relocating.

Career

It doesn't have to be as extreme as leaving your great life in the dust, working two jobs, or depleting your life savings. Deepah, twenty-five, a freelance writer, took more of the middle ground approach as she tried to balance her long-term boyfriend, Ethan, with her plan to go to graduate school. Deepah says it's been a dilemma for her, stating that, "I'm not quite sure how to juggle the relationship and career aspects of my life when they are both so in limbo." Deepah and Ethan are facing the conundrum that so many A Little Bit Marrieds struggle with: How do you weigh your career goals and aspirations before anyone has said "I do"? For Deepah and Ethan, this question was answered by finding a sweet spot—a situation where they each felt they could pursue their individual career aspirations while still building their relationship. The compromise was that Deepah would apply to some graduate programs at schools to which Ethan was also applying, and they came to an agreement that if they got into different schools they would make every effort to choose ones that were close enough to make seeing each other on weekends feasible.

For every Deepah and Ethan that is puzzling how to fit careers and relationship together, there are scores of A Little Bit Marrieds who think that making any kind of career adjustment for someone with whom you are only boyfriend-girlfriend is foolish and shortsighted. Robert, twenty-five, said he's not factoring his girlfriend of two years into his plans to go to business school across the country: "I told Caroline from the first few months that we were dating that this was my plan and that we'd probably need to take a break when I move out there. At this point, I'm not comfortable with having her move for me."

Similarly, Mirra, twenty-three, made the decision to leave her long-term boyfriend in Boston for a great opportunity in California. She said it was a tougher decision to make than she had anticipated, but ultimately she came to the conclusion that passing up this once-in-a-life opportunity would have stymied her career and taken a toll on the relationship by creating resentment.

Relocation

Then there are those who relocate to new cities, trek thousands of miles, give up dream jobs, and then wistfully say, "If I had not been in this relationship, I would be living in Dharamsala." After college, Aaron's girlfriend, Sasha, made the bold decision to move across the country to be with him. Although this wasn't a completely outlandish step for a couple that had been dating for over two years, Aaron says it forced a conversation about what the 3,000 mile journey meant: "I was upfront with her that she couldn't just be moving for me. She had to be doing it for herself." Aaron says that when she got there initially, things were a bit rocky, but they averted disaster by taking two crucial steps. First, Sasha signed a lease for her own apartment, and this gave them the space and freedom for Sasha to develop her own life. Second, they had a conversation that took some of the pressure off of the whole, "I'm moving just for you." Says Aaron: "We were both clear that I couldn't be her only lifeline in Los Angeles."

Anthony, twenty-eight, took a somewhat different approach when he decided to leave a great job to explore whether his two-year, long-distance relationship had the legs to become something more serious: "I always said I wasn't moving because I knew; I was moving because I didn't know. My thought process was: What's the worst that can happen? I'd leave and move back." However, Anthony's decision put the relationship on the fast track to breakup. In hindsight, Anthony says one of the reasons everything spiraled downward was because of the pressure: "I didn't have a job or friends, so I relied on her for all my support." As Anthony found out, moving for someone raises the stakes. Reflecting on why it took him so long to end a deteriorating relationship, Anthony says it was the voice in the back of his head that kept telling him, "But you moved for her, you have to make it work."

In a similar situation, Carly, twenty-five, moved to a new city where she didn't know anyone to be with her boyfriend, who she'd been dating long-distance for two years. "It was definitely nerve-wracking," she says. "It's not my community, it's his. I was concerned that if we had a fight, I wouldn't have anyone to call or anywhere to go." Carly says she had to acknowledge the full scope of the situation—including the major downsides—so she could adopt a more realistic approach to the move. Gretchen, twenty-seven, moved to a small town in the Midwest to be with her long-term boyfriend. "I hadn't really thought about what that decision meant," she says in hindsight. "We had just come from college where everything had this sort of levity and fun factor." Gretchen says she clung to her boyfriend, spawning a vicious cycle of approach and retreat that culminated in a breakup: "It was devastating. I was living there in this small town with no support system." Ultimately, they reunited, but Gretchen says that that period forced her to pull herself together: "I learned how to survive without him, which, ironically, actually helped me survive with him."

The XX Sacrifice Factor

Deciding when, where, how, or if to make a significant lifestyle change or sacrifice at the hand of a relationship is a difficult and complicated decision. To avoid having an "Oh my gosh what I have done?" moment, think about what you'll need from your partner in order to feel confident making whatever type of compromise is on the table. The codified course of action is that before you move across the country or give up a dream job, it's imperative to communicate. Will you expect your partner to make a bigger commitment to you? Or will you be happy if the status quo remains after you move to Boise, Idaho? And can you honestly say you won't be resentful that you turned down a fellowship in Vietnam so you could be closer to your boyfriend? Even for the twenty-first-century Alpha Girl who was raised on adages like "You can be anything" and "A woman needs a man like a fish needs a bicycle," setting contingencies can sound a little retro, but not being married while making marriage-like sacrifices can be risky business.

Although there's no sacrifice algorithm, what's abundantly clear is that any decision that impacts your bottom line must be made judiciously. The adage goes something like, "a man is not a financial plan."

When it comes to their long-term relationships, are they really compromising career advancement for a guy? Some research indicates that young women are not likely to walk away from a promotion to follow the glimmer of a diamond. New York University sociologist Kathleen Gerson found that the vast majority of young women she interviewed were determined to seek financial and emotional self-reliance, even at the expense of a committed relationship. In her March 2007 *American Prospect* article, "What Do Women and Men Want?" she writes, "Most young women—regardless of class, race, or ethnicity—are reluctant to surrender their autonomy in a traditional marriage. When the bonds of marriage are so fragile, relying on a husband for economic security seems foolhardy. And if a relationship deteriorates, economic dependence on a man leaves few means of escape."[2] Gerson found that almost three-quarters of women surveyed said they plan to build a non-negotiable base of self-reliance and an independent identity in the world of paid work before settling down.[3]

Yet, career compromises are often made flippantly. Maya says this is a lesson she realized the hard, experiential way: "The biggest thing I've learned is that when you are married, you can plan your life around someone; when you aren't married, you can't." Lindsey, twenty-seven, says her "Aha!" moment of "I can't act like I'm married if I'm not" came when she started making financial decisions based on her relationship, namely quitting her job to go back to school on the assumption that she and her boyfriend, Cliff, would get engaged and he would support her. After a reality-check conversation with her sister, Lindsey says she realized what a vulnerable position she was putting herself in emotionally and financially: "I was really planning my life around someone who I shouldn't have been." Epilogue: They broke up.

Move to Topeka?
Leave My Job?
Here's How to Know

The "Should I move/leave my great job/take a pay cut" for someone with whom you are just playing house question is a tough one. Anyone who has made this decision can testify that it requires probing. Yet it's less about the aimless naval-gazing than the pointed questions. Here are the must-asks:

- Does s/he think you are just moving to Cincinnati for a fun experiment?
- Have you communicated what this all means?
- Have you weighed what impact, if any, this will have on your career? In other words, is relocating going to limit some of your options career-wise? Are you comfortable with that?

- Do you have a reason, other than your ALBM, to move? If you don't, how does that make you feel? Does your significant other know s/he is the only reason you are going to Arkansas?
- What would you do if you broke up? Do you have a support network there?
- Be honest: How often do you think you'll be hurling the line, "But I moved here for you and your job"? If you think it will be once a week or more, it's probably time to reconsider your decision.

Start a conversation about how you each view your career aspirations and goals. Is your boyfriend/girlfriend factoring you into his/her career plan? Translation: It's not the best idea to follow him to Poland if he hasn't explicitly said, "I want you to come with me to Warsaw."

Ask yourself if you are you making the decision out of fear that you'll lose the person. And by the same token, ask yourself if you are staying in a bad relationship just because you moved for him/her.

Create a baseline by asking yourself what is the largest career compromise you are willing to make for the other person. Is it going to a second-tier law school instead of a first-tier? Is it living in a city you aren't crazy about? Is it taking a bit of a pay cut? Whatever it is, find that outer parameter.

If you are quitting your job to start your own business, going back to school, or taking time off to travel with the assumption that your A Little Bit Married will be paying some of your bills, is s/he aware of that? Is s/he comfortable with that? Is there some quid pro quo? Is the deal that s/he will help you through your period of experimentation and freedom, and then you'll help him/her?

Do you have a financial safety net in case you break up and that income source doesn't come through?

Have you committed yourself to a lifestyle and living situation that you wouldn't be able to afford if your ALBM wasn't supporting you?

If You Are Walking, Then Start Talking—Literally

If you're moving across the country, donning a yarmulke many times a year even though you're a devout Catholic, or abandoning a six-figure income to start at the entry level, it's probably time to start talking the talk. For weeks—through most of December 2006, and into January 2007—one of the most e-mailed articles on the *New York Times* website was, "Marriage Is Not Built on Surprises." Its lead sentence: "In love, as in other matters, what you don't know may hurt you."[4] The article hit on a truism about many A Little Bit Marrieds: People are walking the walk. They are buying homes, living together, relocating, and taking conversion classes—but they aren't talking the talk.

Many couples, even those who express unbridled confidence about getting married, say, "Oh, we haven't talked about THAT," when asked: "How are you going to raise the kids if you are Catholic and she is Jewish?" "How are the finances going to work?" "What are you going to do if you get into the graduate program you applied for in Michigan? Will she move for you?"

To put it mildly, these topics are too big to gloss over, something Amanda Campo and Todd Johnson, the couple profiled in the *Times* article, realized when they participated in Catholic Engaged Encounter, a retreat with forty-four other couples who were planning to marry in the Roman Catholic Church. Out of the retreat came the startling statistic that when the couples were asked whether they would start a family within a year of marriage, nearly three-quarters said they hadn't talked about it and were in disagreement about the timing.

Hammering out all the nuts and bolts won't guarantee that you'll never have twinges or even huge pangs of regret that you moved to Indiana, left your position as vice president, or got baptized, but it's the best insurance policy you can take out before you do so. Of course, leaps of faith are as common in relationships as "Honey, put down the toilet seat" requests, but there is such a thing as an informed leap of faith. Still, as the article in the *Times* observed, many couples heading to the altar "dodge important questions because they don't want to rock the boat."[5] Andrew, twenty-eight, says he worked hard

not to avoid the rock-the-boat question: Would his South In-
dian girlfriend convert to Judaism? He states that, "At some
moment, I realized that I had to tell her that I couldn't continue moving along if I didn't know, at least on some level, that
she was willing to convert. She told me she couldn't do it on
her own, which should have been a signal to me that this probably wasn't ever going to happen."

How can you limit the number of surprises? Well, you definitely can't do it telepathically. Andrew says the approach he
took was having a series of conversations about what they each
wanted and valued: "It was clear that we both valued family,
and I thought that was enough. But tribesmen in Africa and an
Upper East Side mom can also say that. I learned that you
have to value things in the same way. Yes, we both wanted
families. Hers, though, would live in some small corner of real
estate somewhere in New York and our kids would be raised
by nannies, while mine would live in the suburbs and be
raised by both parents."

But for others, the philosophical route doesn't always work
as well. Daphne, twenty-nine, went against the grain of conventional dating advice and took the rapid-fire approach with
her boyfriend who she has now been dating for three years: "I
wanted to know upfront, before I invested or made any big
sacrifices, that he knew what my non-negotiables were and
vice versa." The A Little Bit Married mantra can fast become
"ignorance is bliss." This avoidance is driven by the fear that
putting issues on the table will reveal something they don't

SIGNS YOU ARE COMPROMISING TOO MUCH

There's a very noticeable inequality in how much
you each are compromising—you've moved three
times and given up two jobs.

You are considering moving to a city you really don't like and it
is a desert of career options for your line of work.

You are noticeably resentful and angry about all the
accommodations you are making.

You are making the compromise based on a fear factor—
that if you don't pull the vast majority of the weight,
the relationship will end.

You've significantly decreased your earning potential, or you've
gone seriously off course from a career-track job about which
you were really passionate.

You've given up financial independence and are now
relying on your partner to pay the bills.

want to know. Hope becomes the brick and mortar of many mock-marriages. They are built on the underlying belief that if we move, convert, change our hair color, or start wearing cufflinks our dreams will morph into a wedding that would be worthy of the pages of *Bride* magazine. However, wishful thinking is a rickety foundation for a mock-marriage, not to mention a real one.

Hope is insidious because it fosters what Michelle Cove, creator of the documentary about single women in their thirties entitled *Seeking Happily Ever After*, calls "falling in love with potential." She says, "I think women are quick to nod their heads and say, 'He is so great except for that one thing,' and then that one thing turns out to be huge." A close cousin of "falling in love with potential" is putting on your relationship blinders, which can create a deceptively rosy view. The beauty of being A Little Bit Married is that you are not married, giving you wiggle room to evaluate behavior patterns, tics, and idiosyncrasies more critically because the stakes just aren't as high as when you are married with children. The double-whammy, however, of "falling in love with potential" and the relationship blinders creates a reflex to ignore signs and behaviors that are harbingers of a lifetime of strife and unhappiness. But A Little Bit Married is not an altar on which to sacrifice your personal, psychological, and financial well-being.

A Little Bit Married Rules

Great Expectations is not only the title of a seminal piece of literature by Charles Dickens; it also captures a fundamental component of being A Little Bit Married. Oftentimes these expectations morph into a series of decisions that jigger career plans and change your mailing address. But before you give your two-weeks notice or put your stuff in storage, it's imperative to communicate about what making these decisions means. Use the list of questions from this chapter as a guide-post.

Acknowledge that there is a his/her element to compromise and sacrifice. In general, Men need to see a clear future together in order to sacrifice for their partner, whereas women have a tendency to base these big decisions about sacrifice on more subjective feelings of love and attachment.

Marriage-lite might be a misnomer for this part of the ALBM life, because A Little Bit Married is rife with marriage-like sacrificing and compromising. This chapter examined the overarching, perhaps even philosophical question, of how much you should be acting like you are married when you aren't. Unfortunately, there is no percentage. What there is, however, is a framework for how to think and communicate about making career and location compromises when you aren't married, but there are facets of your relationship that resemble marriage, or if you think that one day you will be married. The two most common types of sacrifice scenarios that couples encountered were ones involving careers and relocation.

Without rehashing some of the cautionary tales discussed in this chapter about moving to a new city without a plan, a job, or friends, drying up your savings, or setting yourself years behind on the career path, it is important to reemphasize how critical it is to not make these decisions in a vacuum. Ask yourself some hard questions and, to the best of your ability, visualize and try to anticipate how you'll feel if you turn down that software engineering job at Google or spend the next three years in Buffalo. Most importantly, get crystal clear with your partner about what it all means. Yes, playing house sounds innocuous—and even fun—but sacrificing your emotional, financial, and psychological well-being is not.

4
Playing House

———— ❖ ————

The Cohabitation
Commandments

> For two people in a marriage to live together day
> after day is unquestionably the one miracle the
> Vatican has overlooked.
>
> —Bill Cosby

No issue seems to cut closer to the quick of A Little Bit Married than real estate—sharing it, not sharing it, and, sometimes, deciding how to divvy it up. If you've decided to forgo the hassle of schlepping your squash gear across town every time you want to spend a night at your boyfriend's, or believe that it's a good idea to take your relationship for a domestic spin before you commit to spending the next five decades together, or "We are basically living together already, why not split the rent?," then you are not alone. These days, according to the U.S. Census Bureau, 5.2 million unmarried couples—one out of ten—live together.[1] And these aren't only senior citizens who've found love again—the twenty-five-to-thirty-four-year-olds are also driving the trend.[2] In an interview with the *New York Times* about how being married now puts you in a minority, Amanda Hawn, twenty-eight, one of the 5.2 million cohabiters, hit on a popular reason why cohabitation has increased 1,000 percent since the 1960s: convenience. She states that, "Owning three toothbrushes and finding that they are always at the wrong house when you are getting ready to go to bed wears on you . . . Moving in together has simplified life."[3]

Consolidating kitchens, costs, and maybe allaying some fears about walking down the aisle, however, only begins to explain why cohabitation has become the norm. "Normal" actually might be an understatement. You are now in the slim minority of couples if you don't live together before you tie the knot. Pam Smock, a sociologist at The University of Michigan who has done extensive research on the patterns of cohabiters, observes that, "The sequence, as many young people see it today, is that you move in and then you get married."[4]

Although living together before marriage is now commonplace, the gravitational pull toward domestication shouldn't be read as a relationship panacea. This chapter will examine the many dynamics of living together. It will dissect what studies say about cohabitation, looking into the often-referenced cocktail party conversation starter: "Don't people who live together have higher divorce rates?" You'll learn the cohabitation commandments and what women, in particular, need to know about moving in, the common arguments for and against living together, and what signs you should look for and questions you should ask before any new closets are built.

What's both interesting and alarming about cohabitation is that everyone is doing it, but there are surprisingly few resources out there for cohabiters and those considering it. The cohabitation conversation usually gets tacked onto the family values argument about "living in sin." This chapter will certainly address the downsides of living together before marriage, but the purpose is not to wag a finger or advance some viewpoint about cohabitation. Rather, it's to present you with the data points so you can make the decision that's right for you and your relationship. Let's start by looking at what experts on both sides of the cohabitation fence say about the pros and cons of living together without a marriage license.

Cohabitation by the Numbers

- 55 percent of opposite-sex cohabiters get married within five years of moving in together.[5]
- 40 percent break up within that same time period.[6]
- About 10 percent remain in an unmarried relationship five years or longer.[7]
- About 75 percent of cohabiters say they plan to marry their partners.[8]

- The majority of couples marrying today have lived together first (53 percent of women's first marriages are preceded by cohabitation).[9]

Cohabitation: The Good, the Bad, and the Ugly

Is living together a good thing for your relationship? A bad thing? Are you more or less likely to get divorced if you live together before marriage? Does moving in with your boyfriend affect the chances of your getting married? Some women interviewed for this book say that they hoped moving in would fast-track the proposal. But the research on that is inconclusive. Researchers, like Smock, say it's difficult to isolate what effect living together has on your chances of getting married because the majority of people who get married are now cohabiting first. What we do know is that living together is not an automatic divorce sentence for your relationship. Dr. Sharon Sassler, a social demographer at Cornell University who has researched cohabiters extensively, says there is a lot of mythology surrounding cohabitation—the most widely touted being the notion that living together is correlated to higher divorce rates, a correlation she and other experts say is erroneous. "Those statistics," she says, "are outdated and drawn from a population whose higher divorce rates have less to do with the fact that they cohabited and more to do with their alternative lifestyle," referring to a 1970s study that generated the belief. However, more recent studies do signal an alarm bell for a select group: serial cohabiters. Sassler goes on to say that, "Only people who live with multiple partners have higher divorce rates. If you've only lived with one person, you have no greater chance of getting divorced than someone who hasn't."[10]

In fact, there's evidence that cohabitation might even give your relationship an edge. In a 2008 *USA Today* article, journalist Sharon Jayson reported that, according to research done by Cornell University sociologist Daniel Lichter, "the odds of divorce among women who married their only cohabiting partner were 28 percent lower than among women who never cohabited before marriage."[11] The correlation between divorce and cohabitation were driven by multiple cohabiting arrangements. Lichter told *USA Today* about his study, published in December 2008 in the *Journal of Marriage and Family*, reiterating that, "Divorce rates for those who cohabit more than once are more than twice as high as for women who cohabited only with their eventual husbands."[12]

That statistic is only one part of the story. Don't pack your boxes yet.

To get the darker underbelly of cohabitation, it's important to raise the question: Why are so many people living together before they get married? Is it because they can? The exorbitant cost of rent? Because it's fun? Those certainly ring true, but the biggest reason is that, these days, couples want to take a test drive—they want to see what it's like to live with that person before they get married. After all, who wouldn't want to sample what the rest of their lives might feel and look like? Lindsey, twenty-nine, says this is the logic that drove her to move in with her boyfriend of three-plus years: "I'm pretty healthy and work out a lot, but my boyfriend has gained a lot of weight and is smoking. I wanted to live with him and see how these things play out before I decide to get married."

Marshall Miller, author of *Unmarried to Each Other: The Essential Guide to Living Together as an Unmarried Couple,* says this is far and away one of the largest drivers of cohabitation: "It makes a lot of sense why people want to live together. If you are going to be living with someone for the rest of your life, wouldn't you want to see what that that person is like not just on a date on Saturday night, but on Monday morning? And also how they handle the bigger things in life, like money?"[13]

In fact, the "I must share the same address with someone before I get married" belief has become so widespread that academics started studying whether the reason behind so many co-lease signings actually improves one's odds for marriage. Living together offers many benefits, ones that can come in the form of a live-in chef, housekeeper, and carpenter. However, the "try before you buy" mentality might be misguided when it comes to strengthening a marriage. Linda Waite, a renowned sociologist at the University of Chicago, who studies the decision to cohabit, the transition from cohabitation to marriage, and the characteristics of cohabiting unions, says the evidence is pretty clear that you can find out what you want to know without living together.[14]

That isn't stopping legions of people, like Lindsey, twenty-nine, who says with a religious-like zeal, "I want to live with my boyfriend for a couple months before we get engaged." Her opinion on this issue is firm. Like many of her peers, she wants to know how she and her long-term boyfriend operate as a cohabiting couple before any nuptials take place. Similarly, Blake, thirty, who is now on his second round of playing house, says his decision to live together was made in order to gain insight into the mundane, the everyday rhythms of life with that person: "You learn people's strengths and weaknesses in a way you can't simulate when you live apart." There's hardly anything outlandish or unreasonable about what Blake, Lindsey, and the millions of other cohabiters give as the reason for moving in. The rub is that it's misguided to think that sharing real estate will give you a protective shield against divorce. The question is: Are people moving in because they think it will increase their chance of getting married? In a 2006 qualitative study—"Heterosexual Cohabitation in the United States: Motives for Living Together Among Young Men and Women"—Smock found a "substantial gender difference" in terms of expectations and goals. "In brief," she observes, "women tended to understand cohabitation as involving greater commitment to the marriage than men . . . for men, marriage was not necessarily the goal of cohabitation." As for the divorce argument, research shows that the opposite might be true. Some say there is actually a thrill crash for cohabiting couples after they've made it official. Living together doesn't always prepare couples for the reality of marriage, which is punctuated by decisions about joint spending, having children, and visiting with in-laws.

So what's the solution? Some experts, like Smock, say practically living with your partner (translation: keeping your own place but spending a good chunk of time at each other's apartments) can give you the same insight into the other person's habits and idiosyncrasies.[15] Melanie, thirty, is engaged to her boyfriend, Greg. She is in the waning population of people her age who say they won't live together until they get married. Asked if she's nervous about saying "I do" without officially having moved in, she explains: "You know what it's going to be like to live with that person by spending nights together and going on vacation. I didn't think that living together was going to open my eyes to anything."

The Tumble Effect

Erica, twenty-seven, is a poster-child for how ALBMs often tumble into living arrangements. "We never really discussed it. It wasn't a formal discussion, really, it just sort of happened," she says of herself and her boyfriend, who have been living together for three years. Sassler found that the tumble effect is a prevalent subculture among cohabiters. Parsing out what she's found in her research, Sassler explains, "Couples don't prepare for moving in together. Very few have talked about it." And

while it's much more fun to think about what your entertain-
ment center will look like, it's the mundane stuff—deciding
who does laundry and who pays the bills—that are woefully
neglected conversation topics. The prevailing outlook among
many cohabiters is that they'll just organically work out a
schedule and all the housework and bill paying will magically
end up evenly divided. "It's surprising how little discussion of
'we-ness' factors into the moving-in conversation," says
Sassler.[16] She says the takeaway from her research is that couples need to uncork topics like what if they got pregnant, are
they going to split the household expenses evenly, and general
expectations surrounding gender roles and sex.

After the decorating high wears off and the initial excitement of "Yay! We live together!" begins to fade, you may come
to the startling realization that you are living with a person
with whom you've neglected to discuss many important issues
that affect your day-to-day quality of life and overall happiness. These include questions like who does the dishes, who
does the grocery shopping, and who cooks—not to mention
how much alone time you each need. Moving in, as many couples point out, is as much a practical, how-you-run-your-
household decision as it is a romantic one.

This all sounds so manageable. After all, you don't have to
have a degree in arbitration or be trained to negotiate Palestinian-
Israeli peace accords in order to have a discussion about paying the electric bill and cleaning the floors after dinner parties.
Although it sounds obvious that these are topics that should
be discussed prior to moving in together, the problem is the

execution. Couples tend to believe that the household will regulate automatically, but those dishes aren't going to wash themselves. Laissez faire might work on a global scale—though confidence in it as an economic theory is wavering as of late—but on the domestic front experts say it's not the best strategy. At the bare minimum, consider the following:

- How will you split the rent? Will it be down the middle? What happens if one person makes significantly more money than the other? Will you split it proportionally to each of your salaries?
- What if you break up? Who will move out?
- Have you talked about the issues that regulate your quality of life? Meaning, who will be responsible for making sure you don't live in a pigsty? Will your new digs just feel like "the frat house grows up"? Or will it be a Buddhist monastery with strict rules about quiet?

Those are just the first socks in the hamper. Here's what emerged from interviews with dozens of house-players about the commandments of living together.

The Cohabitation Commandments

Thou shall be on the same page. Miller, cofounder of the Alternatives to Marriage Project, says this is where he sees a lot of couples go wrong. "You don't necessarily have to agree one hundred percent about the reasons you are moving in together, you just have to be clear with each other about your reasons."

Thou shall truly like the person with whom you move in. Avery, twenty-eight, says her commandment is to strip yourself of any idealization or illusion of that person: "Living together isn't always wine and roses, so you have to truly like that person as a friend."

Thou shall expect the first six months to be rocky. Although no great argument can be made for the artistic quality of the MTV reality show *Newlyweds*, which chronicled Jessica Simpson's and Nick Lachey's train-wreck of a relationship, it highlighted a universal truth: Living together, especially at first, is hard. Asif, twenty-eight, says that even if you try to disaster-proof the move-in by talking about expenses, domestic responsibilities, and promise to count to ten before saying anything after a fight, there's no getting around it: The first six months are challenging. He shares that, "I'd tell anyone moving in together that they aren't going to be as happy as they think they are going to be for the first few months. You're in a learning curve during that time. After four or five months, it got much better."

Thou shall know to whom the couch belongs. This might sound like a childish or primitive mark-your-territory tactic, but living together is about preparing for worst-case scenarios. Taking it a step further, consider drafting a formal "living together contract." In *Marvin v. Marvin*, a case that went all the way to the Supreme Court of California and brought the word "palimony" into our lexicon, the judge ruled that a woman who lived with Hollywood actor Lee Marvin had the right to financial rewards, establishing precedent that unmarried couples have the right to form contracts. According to the National Marriage Project at Rutgers University, today it's not uncommon to have "living together contracts."[17] For most couples these contracts will probably cover pretty basic things, such as belongings. In the event that you own any real estate or have children or any other living and breathing organism, creating an agreement of this kind is imperative. "Do this before you move in," Miller advises. "It's a lot easier to think about worst-case scenarios when you are in a good mood and still buzzing with excitement about living together."

Thou shall not sweep things under the carpet.   Though you might be able to pull off the passive-aggressive-silent treatment when you don't share a mailing address, it doesn't work as well when you can't go home to your own apartment. Sweeping issues under the carpet creates relationship dust— tension, resentment, and animosity.

Thou shall not become just roommates who have sex occasionally.   Domestic malaise is a common state into which cohabiters fall. It's been noted that routine is the number one killer of a great sex life, and domesticating, by definition, is repetitive. Taylor, twenty-nine, says that when she moved in with her boyfriend some of the romance seeped out: "I think just being together all the time can kill a little of that intrigue that is there when you live separately. Even when it's hot and heavy one minute, it's laundry and dishes the next." Falling into a routine that is boring, stifling, or—even worse—makes you take the other person for granted is not a foregone conclusion of moving in together.

Thou shall discuss finances and come up with a budget. Ever heard the widely circulated statistic that money is the number one thing that married couples fight about? You don't need an official marriage license to make that one true.

Thou shall not move in together to save money. Journalist Sascha Rothschild says that she and five of her closest friends all found themselves in the same predicament as they edged toward thirty: divorced. It inspired her to write a piece for *LA Weekly* about the fifteen steps to take in order to get divorced by thirty. Step eleven is: Move in together to save money. This was her friend Aaron's approach to fast-tracking divorce: "His path to getting divorced by 30 was to move in with his girlfriend way too quickly because it made financial sense. Then, once moved in, they fell into plans and a marriage."[18]

Thou shall not merge.   Moving in together is not an invitation to become symbiotic creatures. Many couples said that domesticating is an easy pathway to codependence. That's understandable: Even though you might be sharing close quarters with your significant other, it's important to find some separateness in togetherness.

The Inertia Theory

Now that we know why people move in, how they should move in, and what topics must be broached before they do, let's talk about why people never move out. Although sharing a living space is commonly thought of as an express lane to marriage, Isabell Sawhill, a Senior Fellow at the Brookings Institute, a nonprofit public policy organization, sees a different pattern. She says that, "What often happens is once you are cohabiting, it's comfortable and there isn't much incentive to get married."[19] And yet there isn't much incentive to break up, either. It's no coincidence that longer-term relationships have burst onto the scene at the same time that cohabitation has become the social norm. The view of many A Little Bit Marrieds is that it's easier to stay put than to think about who gets the dining room table or drawing up custody arrangements for Nalu-the-cat.

Inertia isn't just some theoretical concept that academics coined—it's a living, breathing, often corrosive, and very common dynamic among people who date for long periods of time.

Every week a lucky couple gets the crème de la crème treatment in the *New York Times* wedding section with a full spread entitled "Vows" that details the couple's evolution and progression to the altar. On June 6, 2008, Nicola Kraus, the author of *The Nanny Diaries*, and David Wheir were profiled in a charming piece about the circuitous route their courtship had taken. It turns out that David stayed in a bad relationship with another woman for way too long. His younger brother, John, blamed David's inertia on the real estate market: "It's more convenient to stay in an unhealthy relationship than it is to go out and find a sublet," said John.[20]

Luckily, David didn't let apathy keep him in a cushy apartment with the wrong woman—but many do. In fact, it's such a common state of affairs that University of Denver professor Scott Stanley coined the term "inertia theory" to describe the pernicious effect of lingering sluggishness and sluggish lingering. Stanley posits that living together triggers forces that make it more likely that a couple will get married, even if the fit between the partners was poor to begin with.[21] The pull of inertia is really only mitigated by being brutally honest with yourself. Are you staying with the wrong person because you've heard the real estate market is bad? Does it seem unfathomable to try to disentangle your life—not to mention your belongings—from the other person? Experts on both sides agree on this: Living together bonds people deeply. "It's almost as hard as ending a marriage, even though there aren't the legalities," says Smock.[22]

FIVE Signs that You Should
Call the Movers to Move You IN

1. He's cleaned out a closet for you or you've cleaned out one for him without being asked. Although this might sound trivial, the gesture of ceding space and territory is reflective of a deeper sentiment that this person actively, not begrudgingly, wants to take this step.

2. You are moving in because the relationship is working, not as a last-ditch resuscitation effort.

3. The decision to move in together is NOT a result of any of the following real estate-related conditions: apartment search fatigue, the "why pay two mortgages/rents?" argument, or your leases are both up.

4. You've had at least three conversations that account for a possible worst-case scenario. Particularly this one: "If we broke up, who would move out?"

5. You are 99 percent sure this is someone you'd like to have children with.

FIVE Signs that You Should
Call the Movers to Move You OUT

1. You barely speak, the relationship has become so riddled with tension that your friends are constantly shirking dinner invitations because it's that's uncomfortable to be around you two, and the intimacy in your relationship is waning.

2. Your reasons for staying with this person fall into one of these categories:
1) You don't want to look for a new apartment.
2) You'll be lonely—dating sucks.
3) You'll have to start from square one socially, since all your friends are his friends.

3. The ratio of complaining about living with him to enjoying it is 2:1.

4. On at least one occasion, you've made the following cost-benefit analysis: It's easier to stay in the relationship than it is to break up.

5. You are 99 percent sure this is a bad relationship.

What Women Need to Know About Cohabitation That No One Tells Them

After looking at a large slice of the data, and interviewing experts and real flesh-and-blood cohabiters, it's astounding that every man in America doesn't want his girlfriend to move in with him, since the benefits are so bountiful. He gets a housekeeper (cohabiting women mirror married women in that they end up doing the bulk of the housework), a healthcare worker/nutritionist (again, as in marriage, cohabiting women chide men about staying away from the fries and closer to the treadmill), and a social secretary who keeps them scheduled and reminds them to call Aunt Phyllis on her birthday. Then there's what women get: a second shift of cleaning the house when they arrive home from work, and love handles—women tend to gain weight once they move in with their partners.[23]

The housework and eating habits are reversible conditions, particularly the former. We'll get to that in a minute. More menacing is what researchers have found about the expectation gap among cohabiters. A 2006 study, published in the *Journal of Family Psychology*, reports that men are more likely to enter a cohabiting situation with "maybe I do," whereas women tend not to put that qualifier there as often.[24] "This point is most true when the couple starts cohabiting before there is a commitment to marriage, like an engagement," says Stanley. Adding that although this is true in two-thirds or even three-fours of relationships, in others the female will be the less committed one: "So, like all research, it's an average point."

But generally, taking that average point, premarital cohabitation may be riskier for women because they are entering into relationships that they perceive as being more committed than they actually are.

This research exposes another facet of the A Little Bit Married relationship-stage: misinterpreting actions. "[He] may merely be thinking 'This is great for now, until I figure what I'm doing and who I really want to be with in life'," says Aaron, twenty-eight. He noted that when he moved in with his girlfriend when he was twenty-five, he wasn't even thinking about marriage: "I was just thinking this would be fun and that I loved her." Though Aaron is now engaged to his girlfriend, it underscores how casually couples take leaps without any discussion of what they mean. In short, ambiguity is a long-term relationship's arch nemesis. In her focus groups of cohabiting couples, Smock found gender disparities. She shared that, "We are finding that women still want marriage more than men and the men talk about cohabitation as a test drive, while women talk about it as a step toward marriage."

In their seminal book, *The Second Shift*, Arlie Russell Hochschild and Ann Machung coined this term to describe the afterhours work women do when they leave the office. The Second Shift focused on the domestic bind women face when they have jobs outside the home and then have to come home from a day at the office to cook, clean, and nanny.

What's emerged from research of today's cohabiters, however, is that you don't have to have a diamond ring to get stuck with a second shift. In her study of cohabiters, Sassler found that women defaulted into the role of doing a disproportionate amount of the housework.[25] Jamie, twenty-five, says this is what happened to her when she moved in with her boyfriend: "When we started living together, he expected that I would be his housewife. As an event planner, I was working all day, then working at the events at night, and then coming home to a boyfriend who expected me to clean the apartment at 11 P.M."

The movie *The Break-Up* offers a glimpse into a typical domesticating dynamic. Jennifer Aniston's character, Brooke, is constantly peeved that her boyfriend, Gary, played by Vince Vaughn, won't pull his weight with the housework. Charles Hill, a psychology professor at Whittier College, says that "Brookes and Garys" are all too common. "If you're not living together, it's a lot easier to be equal," he says. "But if you're living together, you're faced with certain tasks and decisions—the laundry, the dishes, scrubbing toilets and how to decide these things. Even when people have liberal attitudes, women do the lion's share of housework," he says. He goes on to say that, "Even with a career, she does less but he doesn't do more."[26]

What's the big deal if you do more of the housework than he does? Just ask Amanda Miller, assistant professor of sociology at the University of Central Oklahoma, who studied how cohabiting couples divvy up housework for her sociology dissertation at Ohio State University. She found that the danger in not talking about the division of labor leads couples to default to the typical gender roles. Inequality is like a fast-growing cancer: that, over time, erodes relationships. "Equality is what makes people want to stay together," says Miller.[27]

You don't need sociologists to tell you that that power-shifts occur when two people move in together and try to merge their lives and negotiate everything from food choices to Friday nights. In the anthology *The Bitch in the House: 26 Women Tell the Truth About Sex, Solitude, Work, Motherhood, and Marriage*, Veronica Chambers discusses the trade-offs of living with someone before marriage in her essay "Getting the Milk for Free." Chambers writes about the "about face" she did on the issue of living together. She attributes her 180-degree shift to a friend who said she wouldn't move in with her boyfriend unless they were soon-to-be married because she didn't want to give up her autonomy—except in exchange for deep, lifelong commitment.[28] She wrote, "Living together was less a step on the way to marriage and more a sacrifice I would make in exchange for something else: something equally great but very different. The kind of relationship I wanted with the man I would live with had to be worth giving up all the richness of my single life." Chambers's essay underscores an important step women going through the mental acrobatics of "Should I or shouldn't live with a boyfriend?" would be well-advised to wrestle with a bit more. Simply, as Chambers asks, "Is this guy worth giving up the richness of your life for?"

Your Cohabitation Cheat Sheet

As you can see, cohabitation is a topic brimming with strong opinions on both sides. To help you sift through them all, here are some of the common arguments and their rebuttals.

Argument	Rebuttal
If we move in, I no longer have to wear my gym socks to work, all my stuff is in one place, and my living expenses have been cut in half.	Convenience, whether it's logistical or financial, is not a good enough reason to move in with someone.
Cohabitation is better for men than for women—they do less housework and get all the benefits of a marital relationship without having to make any kind of legal commitment.	Yes, research shows that women don't do less housework or start eating more vegetables, but that doesn't mean that living with a boyfriend doesn't proffer many other benefits for women, such as nurturing the desire to start building a life with someone and, just generally, strengthening your relationship. Also, even if things aren't tit-for-tat equal, many women might feel there is equity. Compromises such as "she does more things around the house, but he pays all of the bills" are ways to keep the relationship in balance.
Why buy the cow when you can get the milk for free?	This argument assumes that men don't want to get married. But research shows that men think

Argument	Rebuttal
(continued from page 91)	marriage is an ideal lifestyle, and three-quarters of men have married by the time they are thirty-five. Here's another reason why people buy "the cow" in the age of "free milk": They really love "the cow."
People just tumble into marriage because they are living together.	Cohabitation is more committed than marriage. When you cohabit with someone you are making a conscious choice, outside of a forced institution, to be with that person.
Living together could delay going to the altar.	True, but it could make you more confident that you are going with the right person when you do.
You have to live with someone to find out what they'll be like in a marriage.	This could be a misconception. Spending a lot of time together—even if you live apart—can be just as good an indicator of long-term compatibility.
Living together is just like marriage.	Not quite, say those who have actually taken the plunge. Marriage changes your relationship in profound ways that living together cannot simulate.

Cohabitation, Continued

There are entire tomes, sociological journals, organizations, and websites devoted to the topic of cohabitation, and this chapter has certainly left more than one or two stones unturned, particularly on the legal front. Many countries, such as Australia and New Zealand, have policies that reflect the large numbers of heterosexual couples living together outside of the typical bonds of marriage. In Australia and New Zealand, it's not just a binary system of single or married; there's a third option called de facto, which refers to a category of people who live together but are offered many of the same benefits as married people. Laws in the United States, however, have not yet evolved to meet the changing social trend, which can cause cohabiting couples to find themselves bereft of many institutional supports. Given that, the following resources might be helpful:

- *Unmarried to Each Other: The Essential Guide to Living Together as An Unmarried Couple* by Dorian Solot and Marshall Miller. They discuss nuts and bolts like how to set up a domestic partnership, legal and financial protection, and being unmarried with children. Also, check out the organization they founded called the Alternatives to Marriage Project (www.unmarried.org).
- The somewhat more conservative National Marriage Project at Rutgers University put out a report entitled "Should We Live Together? What Young Adults Need to Know about Cohabitation before Marriage" by

QUIZ: ARE YOU READY TO PLAY HOUSE? THE SEVEN QUESTIONS THAT WILL LET YOU KNOW

1. You are moving in because
   A. one person's lease is up and it seemed convenient.
   B. you want to see what it's like to live together before you take the plunge.
   C. it's the result of many conversations you've had about the future of your relationship and you both agree that it's an appropriate next step.

2. You've talked about money by
   A. deciding that you'll pay the cable and he'll pay the electric.
   B. briefly discussing how you'll divvy up groceries, home repairs, and rent.
   C. calculating what you each make, and then creating Excel spreadsheets showing how you'll divide up the expenses. You've also read books and articles about how to be financially responsible when as unmarried people living together.

3. A contingency plan is something
   A. you don't need. You are sure this is forever.
   B. something you've talked about in passing. He said he would move out because you found the apartment.
   C. something you have in writing that outlines how you'll handle the lease, the couch you bought together, and your pet.

4. You see moving in together as a sign of
   A. you don't really know . . . but are just happy that he wants to.
   B. a next step toward marriage, but you haven't discussed it.
   C. the logical next step to moving into a more fully committed stage of your relationship, and you are sure of this because you've had many conversations about it.

CONTINUES . . .

QUIZ CONTINUED:

5. He sees moving in as
   A. a relief that he'll get to move into a bigger space.
   B. a fun thing to do together.
   C. what you do when you see a future together.
6. In terms of all the nitty-gritty, such as cooking and cleaning, this is your arrangement:
   A. You don't have one. Aren't those the types of things that just work themselves out?
   B. In the one conversation you've had about it, you decided that you'll cook twice a week and he'll do the bulk of the cleaning.
   C. You've divided up the chores and pasted a chart on the refrigerator.
7. If you had to pick the main reason you want to move in with your boyfriend/girlfriend, it would it be:
   A. Circumstances just sort of dictated the situation.
   B. You hope it will bring your relationship to the next level.
   C. Moving in is what people who see a future together do.

directors David Popenoe and Barbara Dafoe White-head. Visit http://marriage.rutgers.edu/Publications/SWLT2%20TEXT.htm.

For all your legal questions, turn to *Nolo*, an accessible series of legal books. Look for the one by attorneys Ralph Warner, Toni Ihara, and Frederick Hertz called *Living Together: A Legal Guide for Unmarried Couples*.

If four or more of your answers were A's, this is a moment to take a step back and seriously evaluate why you are moving in together. Your answers indicate that this a decision that's being dictated by circumstance. It's unclear what this step means for your relationship, both in terms of day-to-day functioning and long term goals.

If four or more of your answers were B's, you've sorted through some of the issues that couples moving in together should tackle, but haven't done the full reconnaissance. There are still unresolved issues to broach and questions to ask each other. Refer back to the quiz and use the Cs as the gold standard for moving in together. Think about what steps you could take and conversations you can have with your partner in order to make sure you've given this decision adequate consideration.

If four or more of your answers were C's, congratulations, you are ready to move in! You've likely done the necessary preparation for this important decision.

From Heidi and Spencer on the hit pseudo-reality MTV show *The Hills*, to Chandler and Monica on *Friends*, it's clear there's cultural comfort with what once was universally considered "living in sin." Now it's the long-term couples who *don't* live together who find themselves on the fringe. What we know about this fiercely debated—and at times controversial—relationship ritual is that living together does not have a perfect one-to-one correlation with divorce. Research shows that if you do not serially house hop—meaning, you only live with one person—you are at no higher risk for divorce than people who do not live together. That said, it certainly has its downsides. Many couples decide to move in as casually as they decide between brands of breakfast cereal at the supermarket, leading them to aimlessly fall into living arrangements that can fast become emotional squalors. Couples who give cohabitation high marks are the ones who did their homework before anyone signed a lease. Housework, bills, and contingency plans may not be the sexiest topics, but then again, who said living together was supposed to be sexy?

A Little Bit Married Rules

Beware of Free-Falling into a Living Arrangement

It sounds like this: "We never really discussed moving in. It just sort of happened one day when my lease was up." The research is crystal clear here: Those are not ideal conditions under which to start living together.

Laissez-faire Is As Shaky an Economic Theory As It Is a Relationship Theory

Living together requires regulation, oversight, and sorting out questions about who will pay the rent, who will move out if you break up, and how you'll split the housework.

Follow the Cohabitation Commandments

1. Thou shall be on the same page.
2. Thou shall truly like the person with whom you move in.
3. Thou shall expect the first six months to be rocky.
4. Thou shall know to whom the couch belongs.
5. Though shall not sweep things under the carpet.
6. Thou shall not become just roommates who have sex occasionally.
7. Thou shall discuss finances and come up with a budget.
8. Thou shall not move in together to save money.
9. Thou shall not merge.

Be Aware of Gender Roles

Insist on equality when you move in together because just like married women, cohabiting women take on a "second shift" of work when they get home after their paid work to dirty dishes, laundry, and cooking dinner.

5
Are We There Yet?

———— ❖ ————

The Female Proposal

> They say love is blind . . . and marriage is an institution.
> Well, I'm not ready for an institution for the
> blind just yet.
>
> —Mae West

There's an urban legend about a woman who so desperately wanted her boyfriend to propose that she would cut out pictures of diamond rings from magazines and wear the paper version in hopes that one day it would render a real one.

Then there's the calendar approach: One woman marked her calendar with the statement "did not propose" every day that her boyfriend did not propose. Others have turned to physical violence—apparently there's a well-known jujitsu move called "why haven't you proposed yet"—while some go the Sherlock Holmes route, snooping through piles of receipts looking to find a large one from Tiffany's. It's official: You don't need to be a bride to be a 'zilla. While most women don't go to such extremes, any woman who has been in relationship purgatory can probably relate to wanting to take some drastic measure. In the months leading up to the proposal from her now-husband, Gail, twenty-nine, describes herself as having been "possessed": "Here I was, this intelligent person with a great job, a close family, and all these friends, and I was so obsessed with when he would pop the question." Gail ultimately turned to the mightiest of tactics: verbal communication. She told her boyfriend: "Propose to me by your friend's wedding this summer or you're going stag." He proposed six months later.

Doesn't this all feed into the clichés that women want to get married, and men don't, that women have to force men onto one knee and then drag them down the aisle as they tearfully say goodbye to their days of blissful bachelorhood? Well, even in 2009, women still want to get married. Although these days we are looking for more egalitarian models of marriage and are not opposed to starting a family without a husband, for most women it's still a major life goal, and the veracity of this point has surfaced both qualitatively—through interviews for this book—and quantitatively. On the quantitative front, a 2007 survey entitled "What Do Women Want?" was conducted by NBC Universal and Meredith, a leading women's media and marketing company. This survey examined three generations of women's sentiments about relationships, family, careers, and overall life satisfaction: Boomers (born 1943– 1964), Generation X (born 1965–1976), and Generation Y (born 1977–1989). It found that Gen Y women, the main sample for this book, are more likely to place a high priority on marriage compared with other generations.[1] In fact, 72 percent of Gen Ys said "getting married" was an important lifestyle choice to them, compared with 52 percent of Gen X. Though one interpretation of that data is that more Gen X women are already married, so not as many of them place a priority on a goal they've already accomplished, the subtext is that the vast majority of Gen Y women are not eschewing the institution of marriage.

And, for that matter, neither are men—they just don't always want it on the same timetable. When it comes down to the numbers, a 2005 poll, "Coming of Age in America," which surveyed Gen Ys, found that women definitely had the edge on eagerness: 55 percent said they'd like to be married in the next five years, compared to 42 percent among men.[2] And voila, there you have the marital-readiness gap.

Whether it's one year, two years, or ten years, most couples hit a point where permanence or commitment comes into question, and it's not always at the same time for each person. For Irena, twenty-eight, it was at year four. Irena started dating her boyfriend in her mid-twenties and describes the first three years of dating as just "having fun." But then something that she describes as "inexplicable" snapped at forty-eight months: "I suddenly become completely preoccupied with my boyfriend proposing." However, her boyfriend, Jerome, did not share her newfound hobby. Instead, Irena said that, when the she broached the "our future" conversation, he emotionally shut down. "He would clam up when I brought up our future," she said. "Even more frustrating was that he couldn't even explain why he didn't want to talk about it." The months that ensued were tense, as Irena brought up the topic that had previously only been obliquely hinted at. She shares that, "We ended up breaking up for a bit and then getting back together. What followed were many conversations about how to plot our future." Time and space, Irena said, gave them each some much-needed perspective. She came to the conclusion that she would go the ultimatum route: "Marry me or we break up." He proposed seven months later.

Let's acknowledge that there are plenty of women out there who are being pressured by their boyfriends to set a wedding date, don't want to get married at all, or have done their version of getting down on one knee. However, that is not the prevailing storyline that emerged from the interviews for *A Little Bit Married*. What surfaced was that, at a certain point, being in a long-term relationship can feel like you are driving aimlessly on a road trip, and then when you turn to your copilot to help you navigate, he gets huffy and annoyed that you want to highlight a route on a map, instead asking "Why can't we just keep going like we are and see where we end up?"

Exploring the "female proposal" means asking some tough questions, such as, Where is this going? How do you survive in a relationship that doesn't have a compass? How long should you stay A Little Bit Married? Is it after six months? A year? Three years? In any long-term relationship, there will inevitably be questions about the future. When, if ever, should you give an ultimatum?

In her memoir, *I Do But I Don't*, Kamy Wicoff describes the preproposal dance as an exercise in approach and retreat: "A woman wants to get married. Her man complains of pressure. He makes it clear that under such circumstances he can't, delivering, by the way, the male version of the ultimatum—stop pressuring me or I'll never propose . . . The woman in question is then supposed to cease all marriage-related pressure, dedicate herself to work, assume an attitude of cheerful busyness, and generally shut up. If she does, she'll get the ring."[3] Wicoff, then, hits on a certain style of the female proposal. For example, Carly, twenty-five, says she would never want to pressure her long-term boyfriend into proposing, stating, "I know I'm being passive about the situation, which definitely has its drawbacks, because I do have a marriage time frame. I'm just trusting that things will work out." In this case, Carly says her approach isn't about living in some relationship fantasyland where the cosmos align based on wishful thinking, but rather that pushing the issue makes her squeamish: "I don't feel like he's afraid to make a commitment to me. He is always talking about our future and what it will be like when we are married and have kids." Every relationship has its own climate that only the people in it can gauge. Still, most women inevitably start wondering, where is the ring?

To be clear, though, this is not a chapter about how to get your guy to propose through trickery, manipulation, or harassment. "Are we there yet?" is a catchphrase for the cocktail of anxiety, uncertainty, and loss of power many women feel about the future of their relationships. It's a layered question that's more complex than just being an impatient girlfriend—that archetype with which pop culture has had a field day. Yes, impatience is certainly a factor, but hardly the only one. The female proposal is riddled with ideas about adhering to arbitrary timelines, feelings of inadequacy that stem from "not being chosen," and enacting gender roles that often seem archaic. Gender studies professor Michael Kimmel framed the issue well with the question, "If you want to create a relationship for this post-feminist age, how can you do it without relying on outdated dating mores?"[4] This chapter will help you sort out the stew of issues that the female proposal brings to the surface, provide some insights and suggestions about how to talk confidently about the direction and future of your relationship, and examine how and why you need to first propose to yourself. Here are some thoughts.

Welcome to Engagement Purgatory

Whether it hits you at the brink of wedding season, or on a rainy Tuesday afternoon when you're watching the TLC show *Say Yes to the Dress*, or as the 345th person asks you when you and your boyfriend are getting married, engagement purgatory can start to take a toll on your health—not to mention wreak havoc on an otherwise good relationship. Gail describes the months leading up to her boyfriend's proposal as "a war zone," with every battle being waged over "Why haven't you proposed?" For many women, like Gail and Irena, A Little Bit Married can feel like a lot of waiting around, but passively biding your time while hoping for a guy to be ready can all feel—in a word—retro. The hardest part for women in this state of limbo, though, may not be ceding their feminist ideals, it's the lack of power women have in the proposal process. "The pre-engagement period can feel like you don't have control," says Lucy, twenty-seven, who summarizes the sentiment of many other women.

With the power balance all out of alignment—in case you forgot, the standard procedure is still that he asks her—the pre-engagement stage can turn otherwise brazen women into shrinking violets. Michelle Cove, a married documentary film-maker and creator of *Seeking Happily Ever After*, a film about single women in their thirties, says that going from brazen to a potted plant is a play-by-play description of what happened to her when she was A Little Bit Married: "I wasn't very clear about what I wanted. I was afraid to have that conversation. I thought I'd scare him off. But the reality is that you compromise if you don't put it on the table. If you don't ask for it, it's never going to happen. Think of it this way, you weren't going to trick him into it."

Women doing the pre-proposal jig learn a new lexicon that runs the gamut from the garden variety—"Set the date!"—to learning how to ask without asking a question. While men are one-trick ponies when it comes to popping the question—they just have to ask "Will you marry me?"—the female proposal comes in a variety of hues. Here are six different shades.

THE FEMALE PROPOSAL

Type of Female Proposal	What it sounds like
The Basic	"Where is this going?"
The Desperate	"Set the date, set the date, set the date!!!" or "Why won't you marry me?"
The Hypothetical	"So, hypothetically, if you were to get married, when would you see yourself doing that? I'm talking hypothetically; I'm not talking about us or anything. I'm just curious."
The Beat-Around-the-Bush	"I've always thought it would be nice to get married in a barn and have my bridesmaids wear earth tones and the groomsmen wear straw hats. What do you think?"
The Pressured	"I'm twenty-eight, my best friend just got married, I'm in five weddings this summer, you're thirty, isn't it time we got married?" or "Your mom really wants grandchildren."
The Empowered	"I really deserve to have longstanding love in my life—I want it to be you. If you don't feel the same way, I need to know."

Proposing to Yourself

Are you more enamored with a time frame of when you "should" be married than with actually marrying your boyfriend?

Yes, people are getting married later, but that also seems to have intensified the matrimonial pressure in your late twenties and thirties. In *One Perfect Day: The Selling of the American Wedding*, an illuminating investigation into the consumer culture of the wedding industry, author Rebecca Mead notes that, "While the distinction between unmarried and married life has become much less momentous, the wedding itself has become far more so.[5] Mead gets it right: Many A Little Bit Marrieds spoke about the marriage as if it were a side note or a minor afterthought. It was the wedding that they were after. In fact, it was hard to tell whether long-term daters—yes, these were mostly women (the wedding industry doesn't target men with as much gusto)—wanted to get married or if they just wanted to throw a lavish party. The wedding—and by proxy the billion-dollar wedding industry that purveys it—has done a number on our minds, making the wedding into the most sought-after event of adult life. Couple that with the cultural and biological pressure women feel to get married and you've got enough pressure at twenty-nine to launch a small rocket ship.

But somewhere between the panicked longing for a princess-cut diamond and a wedding that would make Colin Cowie proud, we forget to pop the question to ourselves. It sounds like this: "Is this what I want?" Gabby, twenty-eight, says she deflected proposing to herself by just shining a strobe light on whether her boyfriend wanted to get married: "I remember we were out to dinner, it was right around my twenty-fourth birthday, and I asked Jason point-blank, 'Are we going to get married?' He said he wasn't ready. I got really upset. In retrospect, I see that I didn't ask myself that critical question of whether I wanted to marry him." Consumed by the social pressure of matri-mania, women overlook this, the most crucial question: "Do I want to marry him?"

Marrying a Timetable

It's hard to say what's a bigger trigger for the "Where is this going?" conversation—being wedded to the idea of being wedded or arbitrary timetables. Jill is A Little Bit Married—and approaching her fortieth birthday. She says she'll probably get married to her boyfriend of four years one day, but isn't in any hurry, as evidenced by her bio-data. "I've seen people do serious damage to their relationship by forcing it along too fast," she says. "You have to listen to your own timetable and your own rhythm. I've seen friends that got married in their twenties because they felt a lot of pressure, and now they are divorced." Marching to your own wedding beat probably means that you'll deviate from the time frame that society, your mother, and swaths of friends deem appropriate, but you can't marry a calendar. And for many couples, like Molly and her boyfriend, Jake, prolonging marriage has been the right move.

Molly, twenty-seven, says she is taking her time because she wants to be confident that she's making the right decision: "Marriage is a serious commitment; walking down the aisle should be a result of careful consideration and acceptance, not the result of societal pressures because a certain amount of time has passed."

As outlandish as it might sound in the matrimonial pressure-cooker that many women start to inhabit during their late twenties, there's a very popular school of thought that advocates not getting hitched until you are—gasp—thirty years old. Jane Ganahl, a former columnist at the *San Francisco Chronicle*, who wrote about unmarried life, espoused this philosophy in a piece that looked at findings from a Lifetime Television survey. The survey found that Gen Y women, loosely defined as those born after 1980, wanted to get married in their twenties. Thinking about her own twenty-something daughter, Ganahl wrote, "Twenties? The thought makes me shudder. I always told Erin I'd pay for no wedding until she was 30, so convinced was I that no one knows herself well enough in her 20s to make a marriage last."[6]

The point isn't that you should stay in a dead-end relationship or tune out your desire to make a legal life-long commitment to your partner, but there's a lot of space between dead-end and becoming consumed with the proposal. Gail explains that this is the trap into which she fell: "I just moved to New York and instead of exploring the city, I was just obsessed with him proposing to me." Maya, twenty-seven, said she let the marriage dream control her life until she totally lost sight of everything else. The irony here is that sticking to a timetable does not always produce a proposal. Although Mary, thirty-one, is now engaged, her twenties were rife with marriage anxiety: "I walked around with the 'I want to get married face.' When I loosened my grip and took the pressure off feeling this is what should happen at this point in my life, that's actually when it happened."

This isn't to minimize the pre-proposal anxiety (PPA), or to say not thinking about it is a good solution that will result in a proposal. PPA is a real and palpable mental state. And it doesn't all stem from feeling like you are the last of your friends to have a bachelorette party. You want the person with whom you've spent the better portion of the last one, three, five, or seven years to make a bigger commitment to you—and why wouldn't you? But it's so easy to get sucked into the marriage vortex, where even the most levelheaded among us can become fixated on "the proposal" instead of the marriage.

"When Are You Guys Going to Get Married?"

Not only is there internal pressure, but there's often a gaggle of relatives, friends, and coworkers asking and nudging about the impending nuptials. Erica, twenty-seven, recalls that it wasn't just her internal voice that was the problem, but rather everyone else's: "I think what's difficult about this state of limbo is the whole perception of the question 'when are you guys going to married.' I know for my relationship, it put a huge strain on it. We just don't want to plan a wedding right now. It isn't a priority for us." Michelle, twenty-nine, says her ex-boyfriend, who she lived with for five years, received a huge amount of pressure about proposing—and not just from his family, but also from his colleagues: "He worked in finance, at a very white-shoe bank, and it's sort of assumed that you can be 'counted on' more if you have a wife, so he was getting it from all sides."

How do you deal with the marriage-mongers? These responses, A Little Bit Marrieds said, quieted the cacophony of voices.

- We are waiting till we have kids to get married.
- We are married—just not all the way.
- We are waiting till marriage loses its patriarchal baggage.
- We are trying to keep our emotional and financial relationships separate.

The Biological Clock

Charlotte, twenty-nine, lives with her boyfriend of almost a decade, and although she isn't sure how she feels about the institution of marriage, she is certain she wants a family. "My concern, really," she says, "is less about setting a date and more my fertility timetable. I would love to have a family." This brings us to the elephant in this chapter: the biological clock. The arc of a woman's life is very different from a man's, a biological variance that has implications for the female proposal and a marriage timetable. Even though there is some evidence of a male biological clock, as Lisa Belkin reported in the *New York Times Magazine* in April 2009,[7] it did not precipitate a mass rush down the aisle. There's no getting around it: The fertility window can recast your marriage timetable in a very different light. A woman of twenty-eight, with a decade, give or take, of childbearing years ahead of her, is not in the same position as a woman of thirty-eight who wants to have children next month. Many women are having children well into their late thirties and forties, but why waste your prime childbearing years on a guy who isn't sure he wants to be their father?

The cautionary tale goes something like this: Kara, thirty-six, dated her boyfriend, Ed, for five years, the amount of time it took them to figure out that the relationship could not fully launch itself into a marriage. Kara says she doesn't regret the five years they had together, but bemoans the fact that those fertile years are sacred time and she spent them on the wrong guy. Thanks to the amazing advances of medical technology, giving birth in your forties is not fanciful science, but the science here is pretty clear: The older you get, the tougher it is to conceive.

Medical advances aside, Kara hits on something important about "sacred time." If you want to have children, your childbearing years should be hallowed and not squandered on some guy who is still waffling at year four about whether he wants you to be the mother of his children—because there is someone out there who does.

The Ultimatum 2.0: Empowered Conversation

At the dawn of the twenty-first century, the ultimatum is in the midst of a makeover or, at the least, in desperate need of a facelift. The old-guard view of it as an act of desperation does not completely jive with how it's being used today. The ultimatum is a power tool, says Dari, twenty-eight, who has had many "Where is this going?" conversations with her boyfriend: "It wasn't some last-ditch effort of mine, it was a way for me to state what I want and need from the relationship."

The 2.0 iteration of the ultimatum goes something like this: When she was in her mid-twenties, Ashley, thirty-eight, found her best route was not popping the female question, but making a clear statement. She says that, "I told my boyfriend, who is now my husband, that I'd gotten into graduate school, and I wanted him to move with me, but I want us to be married before we did." It didn't sound like an ultimatum because it was simply a declaration of her needs. The consensus among those who have made it out of relationship purgatory is that although sometimes it's uncomfortable and out of your emotional range to talk about the future, knowing is always better than not knowing. Diana, twenty-nine, after getting out of a year-long relationship that she thought was headed toward marriage, decided that being coy was not working. In the relationship that followed shortly thereafter (with the man to whom she is now married), Diana was clear from the outset: "I had been in a situation where I was timid and scared about bringing up the future. That's why with Jeremy I was clear from the beginning.

I told him that I didn't want a boyfriend. I was looking for someone to build a life with. I wanted to be very sure that we were on the same page because it's like that one time you got on the wrong train and ended up in the middle of nowhere, so you want to double-check to make sure that you aren't going to end up there again."

Beth, twenty-eight, also took the direct approach, and is now married to the guy she dated for a little over three years. She shares that, "After about two years, I told Alex, 'I want to marry you and you probably want to marry me, so let's talk about how to make that happen.' I couldn't really be in a state of unknown any more." Although that one conversation did not culminate in a proposal, it uncorked the issue. "It was a jumping-off point," Beth says. "It made me feel that we shared a common vision and I wasn't just wandering aimlessly alone." The new ultimatum has become a way to empower women to have more of a voice in setting the marriage timeline.

Finding the Courage to Ask

Why is it that we have so much trouble asking for something that's so important to us?

Journalist Laura Sessions Stepp, a former *Washington Post* reporter specializing in young people and sexuality, recalled a situation with a graduate student of hers, Selena, who was dating a guy for two years and living with him, but had never talked to him about marriage. "I was floored when I heard that," she says. "We need to think about how we are teaching girls to stand up for their feelings. Why can't they do in a relationship what they can do in other walks of life?" Exactly— why is that? One theory is that we are still living under the thumb of stereotypes and fears of being seen as pushy and aggressive. Dr. Sarah Whitton, a psychologist at Boston University, says to keep in mind that there's a double standard here: "Let's say you give an ultimatum and tell him you'll only move across the country if you have a ring on your finger—that is seen as totally unacceptable and aggressive for a woman, but just a variation of assertive for a man."[8]

Sari, thirty, dated her boyfriend for six years before he proposed. During that period, she popped the question many times, an experience she describes as both humbling and empowering: "Yes, I felt emotionally exposed, but I was proud of myself for being brave enough to give myself permission to want to know where our relationship was going." Cooper Lawrence, a psychology expert and host of the nationally syndicated radio program *The Cooper Lawrence Show*, said she had a very frank conversation with someone to whom she was A Little Bit Married in her late twenties. "We'd been together for a while," she says, "and I asked him if he saw a future with me. He said, 'Sometimes I do and sometimes I don't.' At that moment, I said 'I am out of here.' I wanted someone who was a hundred percent sure."

The Y Chromosome Weighs In

What do men think about the female proposal, ultimatums, and marriage timetables? Conventional dating wisdom says that applying even the smallest amount of pressure to a man is a relationship faux pas commensurate with jumping into bed with someone on the first date. Yet many men interviewed for this book said that a little proposal push is often what they needed. In fact, if women didn't nudge along relationships, the birth rate would probably drop significantly. Michael, twenty-eight, has been dating his girlfriend for four years. He says that some prodding would speed along his proposal timeline: "If my girlfriend gave me an ultimatum of now or never, I'd propose." Asif, twenty-eight, is engaged to his girlfriend of seven years and says that without some pressing, he would have continued to stall: "I was comfortable with letting things be."

As with anything, though, it's all in the approach and the timing. Above all, being direct is critical. Mentioning that you'd like a chocolate wedding cake, you abhor pear-shaped rings, or that October is the perfect month for a wedding are not conversation starters. John Molloy discovered this when he interviewed 2,500 couples of all ages and backgrounds for his unfortunately titled book, *Why Men Marry Some and Not Others*. He shares that, "Many guys said that they went out with a girl for three to five years, and didn't propose because she never brought the subject up, or she did but by then it was too late. Women drop hints—guys don't get hints. You have to say it straight out!"[9] Neil Chethik, the author of *VoiceMale* and an expert on male psychology, agrees that women shouldn't feel they have to be shy when it comes to the "The Future" talk. He does suggest, however, that women frame the conversation in terms of action-oriented questions like: "What would you like to do?" or "What do you think?"[10]

YOU SHOULD
POP THE QUESTION WHEN . . .

it will soon become biologically challenging for you to have children.

the only thing holding you back is that you are afraid to ask.

you want to spend the rest of your life with this guy and
signs indicate that the feeling is mutual.

YOU SHOULDN'T
POP THE QUESTION WHEN . . .

you feel some artificial pressure to get married, like your three best
friends got married last summer or you always thought
you'd be engaged at thirty.

you are riddled with fear about dying alone.

your boyfriend seems unenthusiastic about the relationship. In fact, he's
been sporting that "begrudging" look now for about two years.

RULES FOR THE FEMALE PROPOSAL

Frame it in terms of respect.

If you give an ultimatum,
be prepared to follow through.

Be clear and kind—remember, this is someone you love.

Listen to your gut, not the "I need to get
married by a certain age" mantra.

How to Survive Almost-Engagement

What women said they found the most frustrating and anxiety-producing about this time period was waiting—an act of giving up control. Though it certainly takes Herculean effort, try to focus on the areas of your life over which you do have control—remind yourself that your relationship has many more dimensions than just getting a ring or having a wedding. There are other reasons to be together.

The Almost-Engaged Rules

Waiting for him to propose is not an excuse to act batty.
It's unacceptable to use physical violence, spray paint, or any small, concealed weapons.

Make a concerted effort not to erode your prospective union and current relationship while you're in relationship purgatory. Yes, it's stressful, especially if you've had PPA years, but remember this is someone you love and hope to build a life with, so act accordingly.

Don't compare your situation to another couple's. Marriage is not a track meet. It doesn't matter who gets there first.

Set firm deadlines about how long you'll stay in purgatory.

Smug Marrieds

In the novel *Bridget Jones's Dairy*, Bridget coins the term "smug marrieds" to capture the self-satisfied, superior, and haughty attitude some married people often project, particularly at dinner parties when you are the only one without a date. The "smug marrieds" are another strong force at play in the female proposal—that unsettling feeling that you are the last of your friends to join "the marriage club" can be spooky. Leah, thirty, says it was the summer that she was in seven weddings that put her over the edge: "You feel left out that everyone else is getting married and you aren't." But it isn't just feeling envious of the actual wedding—it cuts to something deeper in women about "being chosen." Leah says she came against these feelings that summer, explaining, "I thought I wasn't good enough or he doesn't want to marry me, and it was just so hard watching all of these other people who had 'been chosen.'" Epilogue: They got married. Leah faced what many women also face—the unpalatable mixture of anger, embarrassment, hurt, and resentment when you feel you aren't being "chosen." In short, the process of being proposed to is more loaded than most shooting rifles. Although it's a huge step for two people to make the highest commitment our society currently offers to heterosexual couples, there's also the strictly female component: The proposal process forces women into waiting to be asked. Although some find that this ritual works for them, for others it increasingly feels like an outdated charade.

The Ring Reckoning

Here is one thought about how we could change the proposal process: Although the female proposal doesn't come with a ring, it's time to have a ring reckoning. For many women, receiving a diamond solitaire becomes their raison d'être—their reason for being for a certain period of a relationship. Let's think radically for a moment about this tradition that has its roots in a time when women were light years behind where they are today socially, economically, and politically. Women are no longer property that needs to be marked or bought. The ring, very literally, becomes a symbol of the power imbalance. What would happen if women stopped hankering for diamonds rings? What if the engagement ring went where it should be historically catalogued: an anachronism of a time when women were considered something to which an economic value could be assigned? A ring reckoning would not only bring engagements into the twenty-first century, it would give the proposal process some much-needed symmetry and a more equal framework for couples to decide together when they wanted to get married.

Does It Really Have to Be Either/Or?

A final point to consider here is whether it really needs to be this strictly binary option of walk-down-the-aisle or walk-out-the-door? Are there versions of relationships that can stay in a limbo phase of A Little Bit Married? Yes. Charlotte, twenty-nine, recalls a tough period she and her long-term boyfriend, Neil, went through because she found herself trapped by what she found were two less than desirable options: "The model seems to be either he proposes to me or that I leave him, and I'm not sure I want either option." They've found a sweet spot by living together and putting marriage on the back burner.

The proposal story that gets told to relatives, friends, and referenced in many toasts at the rehearsal dinner usually involves a clandestine operation consisting of a wig, a mask, a three-man mariachi band, and a blindfold, but for many couples the secret backstory is that there was most likely a female proposal that prompted the male proposal. Women, typically, are a bit ahead of the curve on the marriage timetable.

There's a wide range of ways that women propose, but the consensus is that there may need to be a clear statement that sounds something like, "I'd love to spend the rest of my life with you, but if you don't want the same thing, I just need to know." On a psychological level, the female proposal and the pre-proposal stage can unleash demons and can generally wreak havoc on a relationship if there isn't proper damage control.

A Little Bit Married Rules

Propose to yourself. It sounds like this: "Is this what I want?

March to your own wedding beat—there is no "right" time to get married. Tune out the noise about what society, your parents, and friends say about when you should get married.

The female proposal has to be thought of in tandem with the arc of your life and when—or if—you want to have children.

Use an ultimatum—not as a taunt or provocation, but rather as a clear and straightforward way to express what you need and feel.

When possible, find opportunities to break out of the usual relationship script. Communicate with each other about how to make the proposal process feel less like an homage to old-school gender norms, where the woman sits idly by, waiting for the guy to ask.

6
I Do.
Or Do I?

Handling Doubts

> I was looking for a soul mate, now I'm just looking
> for someone I don't want to strangle.
>
> —*Sex and Sensibility*, Liza Donnelly

In an episode of Seinfeld, *Jerry Seinfeld,* the man who made neuroses hip, breaks up with a woman because she slurps her soup. Little did Seinfeld know that he'd usher in the era of the uber-picky dater, where a little chewing with your mouth open, neglecting to say thank-you to a waitress one time, and the "wrong" Body Mass Index have all become dumpable offenses.

Take, for example, Chelsea, thirty-six, and her boyfriend, Taylor. "He was filled with doubts and was always questioning whether we were really compatible," she said. As for how he perceived their incompatibility, Taylor was flummoxed over how he could marry someone who disagreed with him about what a fun vacation entailed. Alas, they broke up over scuba diving.

But if being A Little Bit Married is all about donning an eyes-wide-open facial expression, shouldn't you be putting your relationship under a microscope? What should you be looking for? Are certain behavior patterns more important to pay attention to than others? Is the fact that your boyfriend consistently forgets to bring you green sauce for your burritos a harbinger that he won't be a loving and generous husband and father? Or is it just a mild case of forgetfulness? What's clear is that doubts come in all shapes and sizes. Amy, thirty-two, who has been dating her boyfriend for eight years, says her doubts surfaced because her boyfriend, Jared, would root for "the jerk" on reality shows: "That was one of our biggest fights. I thought that he was really selfish." Uncertainty is the most certain thing in a relationship, which doesn't always metabolize that well in a culture that's obsessed with "being sure." As A Little Bit Married becomes an increasingly common life stage, the question stumping many is: What qualities, idiosyncrasies, neuroses, and personality traits should I be paying attention to during this prolonged period of courtship? For example, is her treatment of the waitress really a litmus test? How often he calls his mother? What kinds of friends she has?

Are we griping about whether our partner has the food preferences of a toddler? Or are we studying how a partner handles a personal or financial crisis?

And finally, are we listening to our doubts as issues creep up? Are we giving them too much weight? Or are we ignoring them so we can just follow through with our plan to seal the deal?

"I Do. Or Do I?" captures the ubiquitous process A Little Bit Marrieds go through to ascertain if they're courting the person they should spend the next five or six decades with bound by law. For many, it has become an increasingly arduous routine, given the risky business of marriage. Let's not belabor the statistics except to frame it with it with these two: One in five marriages fail within the first five years.[1] And close to half of all marriages end in divorce.

Especially for a generation raised by Boomers, who pioneered the divorce culture, the notion of "I want to be sure" has reached a climax among young people in the dating trenches. In 2002, we were introduced to the concept of a "starter marriage" by journalist Pamela Paul. Paul wrote about the phenomenon of the millions of marriages—mostly between people in their twenties and thirties—that end before five years without any children. At the forefront, however, is the legacy of our parents' generation of marriages—a history that is molding the dating landscape today. With the memories of custody battles, acrimonious dinner tables, and a general atmosphere of family unrest being a not-so-distant flicker in the past, Gen Ys are resolute about not repeating the mistakes their parents made, thereby breeding a rigorous evaluation process of prospective mates to uncover whether or not they are soul mates.

This chapter will examine doubts. These doubts often gel into the foundation for the question: "Is this person the one?" But in all the anguishing over whether this person is "the one," are long-term daters looking at the right data points? To answer that, this chapter will probe what some of the research says about marriages that work, putting the airy-fairy concept of "the one" into more practical terms. In addition, it will give you some guideposts to help you answer "I Do. Or Do I?"

Marrying "The One"

"You need to be smart; you need to make me laugh. I'm looking for all the qualities I would look for in a really good friend, plus that nebulous factor that produces chemistry and compatibility," says Sandyha, twenty-eight, about what she is looking for in her next long-term relationship. The words "I do" used to be a lot easier to come by. In other decades, in the not-so-distant past, people usually got married for utilitarian reasons—financial security and sex. Stephanie Coontz, a preeminent scholar on the institution of marriage, says that the qualities we now seek in relationships—happiness, satisfaction, and equality—are very new additions to the marriage equation: "I have studied 4,000 years of marriage where people did not expect any kind of fairness or fulfillment," says Coontz. "Some people might have managed to carve out a good marriage anyway, but it also meant a lot of people put up with some truly miserable marriages."[2]

Lucky for us, that paradigm has shifted dramatically. The flip side, however, is that the quest for a soul mate has given way to a high-stakes relationship culture. Now that people marry for love and romantic compatibility, the standards can seem impossible for any mere mortal to meet. Everyone is looking for a partner who has the comedic timing of Conan O'Brien, the charm of Bill Clinton, the athletic prowess of Michael Phelps, the moral fortitude of Nelson Mandela, and looks like a cross between Patrick Dempsey and Javier Bardem.

But how reasonable are these wish lists? There's a well-known negotiation saw that says you can never get 100 percent of what you want in anything, so your criteria shouldn't be this perfect—but there should be equity and durability. Yet many long-term daters are still seeking that 100 percent. Christina, thirty-one, says she had to come to the hard realization that her partner, Ellie, was not going to fulfill all of her desires: "I thought the person I married would meet every need and fantasy. I even thought they'd inspire me to exercise. The reality is that only I can inspire myself to exercise." According to a 2001 survey done by the National Marriage Project at Rutgers University, an overwhelming majority (94 percent) of never-married singles agree that "when you marry you want your spouse to be your soul mate, first and foremost."[3]

The *Hartford Courant* dissected this outlook on relationships in an article called "Are Modern Standards Too High?" It commented that, "Today, Americans look to their partners to be everything: best friends and lovers, protectors and counselors.

They want marriages anchored in romance yet practically organized around family and finances."[4] As Asif, twenty-eight, observes about his peers, "They want to hear their heart pitter-patter every time the girl they are with walks in the room. I tell them that's a recipe for a heart attack."

The Perfect Person

Thankfully that's not everyone's romantic philosophy. Evan, twenty-nine, says the idea of a soul mate reminds him of the Paul Simon song, "Train in the Distance," with lyrics that allude to the idea that there is always something better on the horizon or around the corner. Evan says he'll probably marry the girl he's been dating for the past six years, but it's not because she's his soul mate. He says, "I think it's a silly concept that allows people to romanticize the other. It's just a matter of maturity to see there is no perfect soul or perfect mate out there. The person who is constantly holding out for the perfect person is not comfortable with themselves yet." Although the jury is out on whether or not soul mates exist, it's important to remember that no one is perfect. The notion of a "perfect person" is a vestige of an adolescent worldview that perceives the world in black and white. In fact, one hallmark of adulthood is being able to tolerate ambiguity and contradictions in your feelings toward a partner or spouse.

Just ask couples researcher and psychology professor Jim Coan, who says the concept of a soul mate needs to be stamped out like smallpox: "Magical thoughts about soul mates and butterflies in your stomach have been incredibly destructive to relationships. They've created false expectations and set people up for unnecessary disappointment." Sarah Whitton, a psychologist at Boston University, agrees that *soul mate* has brought into modern-day America the false notion that a relationship is a doubt-free zone: Real relationships—the ones that probably wouldn't be the basis for a nineteenth-century romance novel, or movies starring Meg Ryan and Tom Hanks—are based on a yin and a yang, differences, tensions, and areas of incompatibility. The grand irony here is that it's not finding this "perfect," person or "soul mate" that fosters a happy marriage. Legions of experts who research relationships say it's not the soul-mate factor that's the winning formula for a good relationship, it's putting in consistent investments of emotional and physical energy and staying committed to keeping that spark alive.

To be fair, the soul-mate fixation might be a function of youth and idealism. Although there are some compelling arguments to be made for the proverbial "spark," fireworks do not a marriage make. The question then becomes what signs and behaviors should long-term daters be reading into? Are they looking at what kind of parent that person would be? What personality booby traps might lie ahead? Or how they would function running a household together? Experts like Dr. Jeffrey Arnett, who studies the emerging adult population, says these questions are a bit off the dating radar: "They aren't just looking for a practical arrangement for running a household. They are looking for this almost spiritual match." Arnett's conclusion is that intimacy expectations of today's young people are off the charts. "This generation," he argues, "has to come to terms with the fact that they are marrying a human being."[5] The paradox here, as Arnett points out, is the generation—the Baby Boomers—who invented the concept of a soul mate do not have a particularly admirable success rate in their own marriages.

Those who have given up on the lofty and unattainable notions of a soul mate and perfection say it's a huge relief. "In every other relationship, I've looked for a soul mate and been that crazy romantic. I realized that what is more important is that I find someone who, when I'm eighty and going bald, I can laugh with," says Addison, twenty-eight, who lives with her boyfriend of three years. Similarly, Nina, thirty, says being A Little Bit Married and now married modulated her expectations: "I was definitely a hopeless romantic before this five-year relationship. The reality is that being with someone is down and dirty. There is a lot of bickering and figuring each other out and not always being in the same place."

Normal Doubts vs. Deal-Breakers

In a culture that has done such a superb job of manufacturing and purveying the concept of a soul mate, anyone in a long-term relationship will be forced to ask themselves: "Am I putting too many expectations and pressures on one relationship?" Scholars like Coontz, who study marriage, are sympathetic to the woes of twenty-first-century courtship and its less-defined criteria and structure, saying, "I think that today it's hard to know when you are there. How do you know you are really mature enough to get married? How do you know when you are really committed?" It's definitely hard to say. Colleen, twenty-nine, broke off her engagement because she became consumed with doubts about saying "I do" to her fiancé: "I kept asking myself, 'Do I just love him or am I *in* love with him? Should I hold out for something more?'" For Colleen, the crystallizing moment was when her maid of honor leveled with her and said out loud what Colleen had been thinking silently for months: "It's so clear that you don't want to marry this guy." Although Colleen describes her ex-fiancé as "perfect on paper," they didn't "spark," have enough common interests, or share the same values. Her outlook now is that she doesn't want to be with someone unless "they rock her world." Admitting she might be buying into a Hollywood-produced romantic ideal, she says, "I'm just going on the assumption that it does happen and I want to hold out for someone absolutely amazing."

Still, at what point do you let go of someone so you can hold out for someone better to come along, and when do you say, "Yeah, it's not perfect, but the notion of the perfect marriage is smoke and mirrors?" Diana, twenty-nine, who spent a good portion of her twenties drifting in and out of long-term relationships and is now married, says she sees the process as analogous to purchasing real estate: "There are going to be some that are really gorgeous and appealing condos, but you get to a point where you just need a place to live. I found myself on this endless search because there was no such thing as a perfect condo."

Let's be absolutely clear: There is nothing inherently wrong with having high standards or holding out for the right person. What's troubling, experts say, is expecting that one person to fulfill all your needs.

Michaela, thirty-two, says she had that epiphany about a year into her marriage: "I realized that everything he needed wasn't going to come from me." Sociologists at the University of Arizona and Duke University support Michaela's experience with their findings that from 1985 to 2004, Americans reported a marked decline in the number of people with whom they discussed meaningful matters. People reported fewer close relationships with coworkers, extended family members, neighbors, and friends.[6] The result? More and more pressure on your partner to fill the void that used to be filled by coworkers, extended family members, friends, and neighbors. That's why psychologists, sociologists, and educators have been sounding the alarm that because of hyper-individualism coupled with the rise of social networking sites, it's critical to forge bonds outside of your romantic relationship that don't rely solely on an Internet connection.

Are You Putting Too Many Expectations on Your Relationship?

Not all doubts are created equal. There are the hesitations that creep up from seeing your partner's self-destructive behavior, anger management problems, or borderline abusive treatment of small household pets. And then there are the doubts that are a sign of unrealistic expectations. Here are some questions to ask yourself:

- Do you depend on your relationship as your primary source of emotional, intellectual, and social support?
- When you tell your friends and family what you are looking for in a partner, do they tell you that person doesn't exist?
- Are the expectations you are placing on the relationship relevant to the big picture of what you want from your life? Or are you harping on small and insignificant personality quirks?
- Do you equate compromising with settling?
- How many of the qualities you are looking for in a partner would you be willing to negotiate? Or when you take an inventory, do you find that you are intractable regarding your wish list?

The Happiness Factor

We live in a society obsessed with happiness—how to get it, keep it, and reproduce it. However, "Am I happy all the time?" is a misleading benchmark for evaluating your relationships. Diana said she stopped asking herself "Am I happy?" and started asking herself "Is he a partner for me as we go through life together?" She goes on to say, "I'm interested in building a life and having kids. It's not about someone fulfilling every whim and desire, it's about what we can do together. I'm not necessarily going to wake up every morning giggling, but I don't think that's the point."

Doubts, the Receiving End

Doubts are a two-way street, so what do you do when you are the one who is under the microscope? Rachel, thirty, dated her boyfriend for over two years before she moved out on account of his lingering uncertainty. The process, Rachel says, felt like someone was dangling a carrot in front of her: "How was I supposed to act normal while he was waiting for 'this feeling'?" Caroline, twenty-eight, says she went through a similar situation with her boyfriend of eight years: "At around year six or seven, he started having these doubts." Her instructive reckoning on the situation was this: "People personalize a partner's doubts. I came to the point where if he thought I wasn't 'good enough,' he has to figure that out for himself. Too often women think it's something about us. This whole process can't be about some guy telling you are good enough for some stupid ring."

Deal-Breaker Exercise

When Charles Darwin wrote "This Is the Question," a set of notes he drafted between 1837 and 1838, he was not pondering finches. "This Is the Question" represented the evolutionary theorist's attempt to logically evaluate whether he should marry his girlfriend, Emma Wedgwood.

Using his trademark rationality, Darwin made two columns: "Marry" and "Not Marry."

In the "Marry" column, he entered: "Home and someone to take care of house—Charms of music and female chit-chat. These things good for one's health. Forced to visit and receive relations but terrible loss of time. My God, is it intolerable to think of spending one's whole life, like a neuter bee, working, working, & nothing after all."[7]

The antipode to those points, in the "Not Marry" column, was: "Freedom to go where one liked—Choice of Society and little of it. Conversations of clever men at clubs. Not forced to visit relatives, and to bend to every little trifle." For two years, the *Origin of Species* author worked on this dispassionate calculation until finally reaching a conclusion. On January 29, 1839, Miss Emma Wedgwood became Mrs. Emma Darwin.

See, even Darwin had doubts and did a deal-breaker exercise! Doubts are their own organisms with a complex DNA code, and certainly doing a single exercise can seem reductive and one-dimensional. That said, you have to start somewhere. Here are two exercises to help you get a handle on your hesitations.

It's unrealistic that any one person is going to be 100 percent of what you are looking for, so let's shelve that standard. Instead, prioritize what actually is important and then prioritize those priorities. Hayley, thirty-six, says the problem with her starter marriage was that although her ex-husband was 90 percent of what she was looking for, the remaining 10 percent that was missing eclipsed all of the qualities she found appealing. This deal-breaker exercise comes down to knowing yourself. For example, even if the person is almost everything on your list, but s/he doesn't have a sense of humor, will that missing quality be a huge, ominous cloud hanging over your relationship? Would you not marry someone who doesn't believe in global warming? Is pro-life? Comes from a different religious background? Has a temper? Is overly emotional? Get crystal clear about your no-budge areas.

On the nuts-and-bolts side, how do you want your life to look? Do you want to raise kids in the suburbs or in a more urban area? What are your thoughts about gender dynamics and who should work and stay home with the kids? Are they more traditional? Or do you want to split childrearing and running a household fifty-fifty? It's quaint to think that love conquers all, but it doesn't. You have to find someone with whom you can negotiate and compromise on everything from children to mortgages to religion.

Colleen, twenty-nine, says these are issues she wished she had thought about more before she said "yes" to her ex-fiancé's proposal: "I think you can get so blindsided by love that you forget to verbalize what you want." In hindsight, Colleen believes she never made it to the altar because of the areas of incompatibility that she never considered until after she set a wedding date. As their disparate life visions started to emerge—he wanted her to be June Cleaver and she wanted to live in a Bohemian artists' colony—it created barriers that became increasingly difficult to surmount.

Like many long-term daters, Colleen asked herself the tough questions *after* she accepted the diamond ring. She shares that, "I didn't give a lot of thought to how I wanted my life to look, what the gender dynamics in our relationship would be, how we would raise our kids—I just kind of went along with it. It all sounds fine and good, but when you start to realize that's the life you are going to be living, it's terrifying." Sketching out a vision of her own future, it hardly resembled the traditional picket-fence, suburban one her ex-fiancé envisioned: "It was like I was just stepping into someone else's life without giving much thought to what I wanted."

Too-High Expectations

Jean Twenge, a psychology researcher at San Diego State University, made headlines in 2006 with her book, *Gen Me: Why Today's Young Americans Are More Confident, Assertive, Entitled—and More Miserable Than Ever Before*. Her research unearthed many of the maladies brought about by having sky-high expectations. It's why Twenge says to not get carried away with what you are looking for: "Make the list of things you want in a perfect partner and then throw half of them away. Try to be honest and think only about what you absolutely must have." Twenge says the reality check is this: "If you even get close to someone who meets what is on your list, you're pretty lucky."[8]

Where do these high expectations have their roots? Twenge found in her research that young people have bought into the advertising slogan, "You deserve the best," a very popular mentality fostered by advertisements of products ranging from soup to cars. That mantra, Twenge says, should be amended to, "You deserve the best some of the time." But what's wrong with thinking you deserve the best and standing your ground and not settling for less than the best? Twenge found in her research that larger-than-life expectations set people up for disappointment, the on-switch for unhappiness: "In general, there is a disconnection from reality. People expect their partners to make them happy all the time and for that euphoria to last. And none of this is realistic, so they end up really unhappy that reality doesn't mirror the vision they had of marriage in their mind." The reality is a lot closer to the description psychologist Daniel Wile gives in his book *After the Honeymoon*: "When choosing a long-term partner . . . you will inevitably be choosing a particular set of unsolvable problems that you'll be grappling for the next ten, twenty, or fifty years."[9]

How Can You Be Sure You Are Sure?

We all know someone in this category—the people who say "they just knew" when you ask them how they knew their now-spouse was the person they wanted to marry. How realistic is that? Can you really "just know"? Is there such a thing as being certain? Robert Burton, a neurologist, wrote a book entitled *On Being Certain: Believing You Are Right Even When You're Not.* In it, he tackles a question that has puzzled him since his foray into the medical field three decades ago: What does it mean to be convinced? He is now deluged with requests from people seeking help with decision-making. The crux of his argument is to dispel the myth of "we know what we know" and to call into question the conventional wisdom of "I just knew." Burton argues that the brain creates an involuntary sensation of "knowing" that is affected by what he calls our unseen iconography—our genetic predispositions, perceptual illusions, and bodily sensations.[10] Simply put, Burton says certainty doesn't exist: "[Certainty is] not biologically possible," he writes. "We must learn (and teach our children) to tolerate the unpleasantness of uncertainty."[11]

What implications does this have for those of us deciding whether to go from A Little Bit Married to married? Many. Drawing on personal experience, Burton, who has been married to his wife for forty years, says that right after he got married he and his new bride were driving to their honeymoon when he asked himself, "What have I done?" Reflecting on that moment, Burton believes it's a universal feeling: "I think that's what every person says after they get married."

Burton has been happily married for decades, so his question didn't arise because he thought he married the wrong person. The "What have I done?" moment is commonplace—a consequence of what Burton says is the very nature of deciding to get married: "There is no expertise in match choosing, so it makes sense to feel unsure about it." To that point, Burton challenges the conventional wisdom about how to choose a good partner, stating that, "It's just hard to know what is a good decision in advance, even if you account and control for what you are going to want twenty years from now." Mate selection, like any decision, Burton says, is based on a wide variety of factors, including sexual attraction and financial security, preferences that are rooted in a subjective iconography and set of idiosyncrasies.

In other words, there is no relationship forecasting system. If you believe Burton's model that you can't be certain, or the more watered-down version that life will undoubtedly go in many directions that you can't anticipate, the calculus is this: Figure out whether your partner has qualities like resiliency, flexibility, and adaptability. These traits, Burton says, will be the best predicator of what kind of partner you are getting.

How Can You Know If This Person Is the One?

There is no regression model to predict whether the person you are A Little Bit Married to will make a good life partner, but there are certain variables to examine closely. Think of these as relationship booby traps or, in the spirit of Ashton Kutcher, how not to get "punked" in a relationship.

How does s/he react to change or crisis?　Burton says to think about how the person you are with would react if you told them you were quitting your job to write a novel? How would they deal if you came home with a diagnosis of diabetes or, worse, cancer? In general, how do they deal with setbacks? All you can know is whether the person with whom you are contemplating walking down the aisle is well-equipped to cope with what life is certain to bring: uncertainty.

Can you laugh together?　As George Eliot once said, "A different taste in jokes is a great strain on the affections." Burton says his personal relationship litmus test for "I Do. Or Do I?" is humor: "Life is ludicrous, so make sure you marry someone with a good sense of humor. Pick the jokes that you think are the funniest and see if the other person laughs. It will give you more insight into their view of the world than most conversations."[12]

What is your intuition telling you?　What happens if your doubts aren't flashing-light-red obvious? According to research done by University of Austin Texas Professor Ted Huston, who studied 168 couples in order to gain insight into what predicts a happy marriage, doubts should not be brushed aside. Huston's research revealed that women who sensed future problems while they were still courting found out after they were married that their concerns were well-founded.[13] Women have long been lauded for their intuitiveness—and apparently for good reason. When we pay close attention to that sixth sense, it can help us find the right real estate, jobs, and, now, husbands.

Do you feel like you're "forcing" things to work?   Men would be well-advised to listen their intuition as well. Nelson, twenty-eight, took the common "persevere at all costs" approach to his doubts, saying, "I just thought I'd give this the old college try and make it work." Yet, that didn't change the reality that he and his long-term girlfriend were completely incompatible: "If we were to make ninety decisions, we would only make forty of them alike," he says about their divergent worldviews. Although the shopworn adage states that relationships take work, you can't always be working overtime. There absolutely has to be some ease and many areas of compatibility. Ask yourself: If you were to make ten decisions, on how many of them would you and your partner be in agreement?

On the whole, is your relationship getting better over time?   Dr. Diana Kirschner, a psychologist and author of *Love in 90 Days: The Essential Guide to Finding Your Own True Love*, says the key to sifting through your doubts is to view them historically: "What is the trend in the relationship? Is it getting better even though there are highs and lows? Is s/he becoming more available to you? Is s/he sharing more? Am I happier over time with him? You want to identify the overall trend." The tendency, Kirschner says, is to get lost in the minutia of "He snapped at me," or "She didn't want to go out with my friends one night," or "He leaves his dirty soccer cleats on the clean rug." She advises, "Don't put so much stock in the emotional upticks and downticks. Rather, you should be tracking the overall movement. Is this intimacy getting better?"[14]

Does the relationship feel conditional?   Are you afraid that if you expose your backstage personality—the irascible, grumpy, curmudgeon side—that s/he will walk out the door? Or are you able to showcase the full range of your personality and just be yourself?

Do you both stay on the dance floor?   Even when times get tough—one person loses a job, has a bout of depression, or has to take care of a sick parent—does your partner stay engaged? Or does s/he pull away once the music stops?

Is the person erratic?   Is your relationship some version of Dr. Jekyl and Mr. Hyde? Are you always wondering which version of your partner you are going to get? This isn't about normal, everyday mood swings, but rather vast fluctuations that make you feel like the rug could always be pulled out from under you.

How do you fight?   Leo Tolstoy got it right when he said: "What counts in making a happy marriage is not so much how compatible you are, but how you deal with incompatibility."

When problems arise, are you always apologizing? Will you both actively participate in a discussion? Also pay attention to fighting dirty and taking below-the-belt shots. Is there nasty name calling? Are you able to resolve conflicts effectively and then move on?

10. Does this person bring out the best in you?   How do you feel when you are around this person? Does s/he encourage you to pursue your dreams and passions? Or do you feel stifled and stymied? Do you like the person you are in the relationship?

11. Do they take care of themselves?   Does s/he deal with problems in their lives as they come up? If they get depressed or have some other mental hiccup, do they seek the help they need? Do they engage in a lot of self-destructive habits? Try to gauge what priority she or he places on their emotional and physical well-being, because it's an excellent indicator of what kind of treatment you'll receive.

Spat Is Not a Four-Letter Word

In the 1977 Woody Allen movie *Annie Hall*, the main character, Alvy Singer, approaches a happy couple on the street and inquires how they do it. The young woman says, "I'm very shallow and empty and have nothing of interest to say." Then her boyfriend chimes in with, "I'm exactly the same way." Couples

aren't supposed to always be in agreement and, more importantly, a courtship free of conflict should not be interpreted as
a sign that you are destined for martial bliss. Despite this,
many long-term daters are under the impression that tiffs and
squabbles are a sign that a relationship is doomed. But, *au
contraire*. Couples tend to have the same amount of disagreements whether they divorce or stay together. Tiffs over credit
card bills, not being in the mood, an overbearing mother-in-
law, and objecting to a motorcycle-themed vacation are pretty
much the realities of all marriages. The difference between
the couples who divorce and the couples who stay together is
how they fight.

Jim Coan, a professor of psychology at the University of
Virginia, wants to dispel the myth that fighting is bad for a relationship. "It's very clear from multiple laboratory studies," he
argues, "that it isn't. In fact, it's as inevitable as the sun coming
up in the morning."[15] That doesn't mean that you should start
picking fights, or pulling out buried hatchets. Rather, your
time is better spent evaluating your fighting style. Coan
learned that there are some fairly predictable patterns associated with long-term happiness or disillusionment. The couples
who are more likely to be disillusioned were the ones who
raised problems in a very aggressive manner or with contempt.
They were also the ones that made issues an attack on their
partner's character. For example, "You never take out the garbage! What is wrong with you?," as opposed to, "I'd really
appreciate it if you could take out the garbage more often." In

his study, Coan found that the couples that were able to master the subtle distinction between making the complaint behavioral versus character-based were generally happier. The happier couples were also able to master something Coan calls "soothing": They were able to infuse some positive emotion, like a gentle touch or a joke, even in the midst of a tense and heated conflict. This, apparently, is also good for your health. Dr. John Gottman, who runs the "love lab" at Washington University in Seattle, found that couples who are contemptuous of each other are more likely to suffer from infectious illness (colds and flu) than other people.[16]

Dr. David Olson is professor emeritus of family social science at the University of Minnesota and the president of Life Innovations, a company formed out of his research about how to develop an inventory for couples called Prepare Enrich. He has pinpointed some key differences between happy and unhappy couples that he discusses in the book he coauthored with Amy K. Olson, *Empowering Couples: Building on Your Strengths*, based on over twenty years of experience and clinical research with couples. He found that happy couples are more likely to agree with statements like:

- I am very satisfied with how we talk to each other.
- We are creative in how we handle our differences.
- We feel very close to each other.
- My partner is seldom too controlling.
- When discussing problems, my partner understands my opinions and ideas.

- We have a good balance of leisure time spent together and separately.
- My parents, friends, or family rarely interfere with our relationship.
- We agree on how to spend money.
- I am satisfied with how we express spiritual values and beliefs.[17]

There's a hierarchy here. Olson found in his national survey of over 21,000 married couples that the most significant distinguishing factor was whether one's partner feels understood when discussing problems.[18]

Over the years, many researchers have tried to answer the question: What predicts whether a couple after two years of marriage will stay together? Ted Huston, a professor of human psychology at the University of Texas at Austin, entered a crowded field of researchers studying what makes a marriage last and, in the process, shed light on qualities to seek out during a prolonged courtship. The 168 couples were selected from public marriage license records in Pennsylvania and were white, working-class, and in their early twenties. Although the sample is small and it is therefore difficult to draw any large, sweeping conclusions about marital satisfaction from it, Huston hit on some of the key ingredients for a successful relationship: "Marriages in which one or both spouses possess stereotypically 'feminine' traits such as warmth, kindness and a high level of concern for others tend to evidence a strong degree of marital satisfaction and are preceded by courtships that show a smooth, even progression toward marriage. Individuals with so-called feminine traits typically behave more affectionately and elicit similar behavior from a partner, and they also are inclined to give each other the benefit of the doubt."[19]

Becoming a Wife

A final word about the universe of doubts. Michelle, twenty-nine, who lived with her boyfriend for over three years, is emblematic of what a number of women said about marriage—that it would mean turning themselves over to the fun police. She says, "I always had this negative idea about marriage—that it's the end of your life. Most of my friends who are married never go out any more."

There's no getting around it: "Wife" has a complicated history and a checkered past. In 1972, *Ms. Magazine* ran an article called "Why I Want a Wife" about the myriad of expectations and constrictions that are placed on a wife. The punch line of the article, after describing this "wife" who would go to every physical, emotional, and psychological length to please her husband, is: "My God, who wouldn't want a wife?"[20] Although times have changed since "Why I Want a Wife" was published, women still do the lion's share of the housework, and child-care responsibilities are still not divided equally. Young women today aren't tone deaf to what society expects from a wife, and, in the gray zone of A Little Bit Married, they seem to feel less obligated to take on the full load of "wifely" duties. Anne, twenty-six, who is in a long-term relationship, explains, "If I were his wife, I would feel that I would have to cook him dinner. There is so much more freedom being A Little Bit Married. I can work late. I can go out to a party on my own." Whether *Fear of Flying*, Erica Jong's book about a woman conflicted about being a free sexual being or a wife, would have struck as much of a chord in 2010 as it did in 1972, we'll never know. But what we do know is that the meaning of *wife* is still evolving.

Marilyn Yalom, author of *A History of the Wife* and a senior scholar at the Institute for Women and Gender at Stanford University, charted the evolution of the wife from the ancient world to the start of the millennium and gives a valuable perspective for this generation of women contemplating wifehood. She writes, "Americans are not giving up on wifehood." Yalom sets forth both the mandate—and the challenge—for women today "to create more perfect unions on the basis of their new status as co-earners and their husband's fledgling status as co-homemakers."[21]

Les Parrott, a professor of psychology at Seattle Pacific University and coauthor of *Saving Your Marriage Before It Starts*, teaches a very popular class about relationship development. One of his main observations is that, "This generation has so much anxiety about marriage."[22]

There's been no blue-ribbon panel commissioned on how to handle doubts in a long-term relationship, which is why this chapter dealt with an issue that becomes the center of gravity for many A Little Bit Marrieds: Do I want to marry to this person? And as a corollary, if I have doubts, are they normal? Should I be paying attention to them more or less? Are my expectations too high or am I simply being prescient about the fact that this man will one day run off with the eighteen-year-old babysitter and develop a $3,000 porn habit à la Christie Brinkley's ex-husband, Peter Cook? To that point, Maureen Dowd, a *New York Times* columnist, wrote a column entitled "An Ideal Husband," inspired by the Brinkley/Cook debacle, that tackled the question "how to dodge mates who would maul your happiness." Dowd culled advice given by Father Pat Connor, a Catholic priest and marriage counselor, from a talk he gives mostly to high school seniors called, "Whom Not to Marry." Among the many wise pieces of advice Father Connor offers, he gets to the core of "I Do. Or Do I?" with this nugget: "Don't marry a problem character thinking you will change him." He goes on to say, "He's a heavy drinker, or some other kind of addict, but if he marries a good woman, he'll settle down. People are the same after marriage as before, only more so."[23]

A Little Bit Married Rules

Dial down your expectations of a potential husband or wife so that they mirror reality, not an avatar you create on Second Life or some fantasy Facebook profile. Sky-high expectations will inevitably lead to disappointment. This doesn't mean settling, but rather coming up with a realistic sketch of what you want in a mate.

While it can sound methodical and calculated to think about deal breakers or exercises involving lists, sometimes, as Darwin found, it's a valuable way to gain clarity. Get clear about what is important to you and then prioritize those priorities. We all have a "wish list," but not everything on that list has the same rank. Do some introspection about what qualities you must have in a partner and which ones are expendable.

Keep in mind that marriage is an inexact science, but you can be on the lookout for booby traps by asking these questions: How does s/he react to change or crisis? Can you laugh together? What is your intuition telling you? Do you feel like you're "forcing" things to work? On the whole, is your relationship getting better over time? Does the relationship feel conditional? Do you both stay on the dance floor? How do you fight? Does this person bring out the best in you? Do they take care of themselves?

7
Walking
Out the Door

————◆————

How to Go From
A Little Bit Married
to Very Broken Up

> You never really know a man
> until you have divorced him.
>
> —Norman Mailer

   Unlike casual dating, those who are A
Little Bit Married don't usually view it as "just for fun." Endemic to these relationships is often the expectation that it
will produce a life-long commitment. Welcome to the world of
high-stakes breakups. Ending the most significant relationship
of your adult life thus far, a relationship that was "supposed" to
culminate in marriage, can feel like a twisted ending to something you thought would be a fairy tale. "I felt a little bit like
a failure," says Lisa, twenty-seven, about her emotional state

after her three-and-half year relationship ended. "When I started dating again, I was looking for marriage to annul the non-marriage of my previous relationship. What I figured out is that marriage is not the indicator of success and not every relationship has to be about that." Here's where it's probably helpful to get a bit philosophical about the relationship and not view it in terms of success or failure. Since the Facebook generation will probably have a number of long-term relationships before marriage, not every one is meant to end in an elaborate affair.

"Some people say that when you eventually break up with someone, you are just admitting things that you knew all along," says Nitten, twenty-eight, about how he felt after he broke up with his long-term and live-in girlfriend. "It was an incredibly painful process." Ah, the proverbial mirror that anyone walking out the door holds up. Then there are all the practical concerns: readjusting your holiday schedule, revising your social life, and changing your locks. There might be pet custody arrangements, real estate court battles, and War of the Roses-esque drama. "It was like a divorce," says Annie, twenty-six, about the sudden breakup with her boyfriend, Josh, after almost four years together. "Even our friends had to be divided up, and I felt like I lost a whole family."

There's no question about it: It feels awful to split up, particularly if you have lived together. "Every part of your life is going to be affected by it: financially, socially, psychologically, and emotionally. In the context of your world, it's a shake-up of your entire life,"[1] says Kate Wachs, a Chicago psychologist. That's certainly how Jamie, twenty-five, felt, saying, "It's not just about moving out of your home. You have to divide up your life, your friends, restaurants, and bars." Although not everyone chooses to be so Solomonic about splitting up, Jamie said that's what she needed to start going forward.

Kara, thirty-six, recalls the months after her five-year relationship as akin to mourning a death: "Spending every day together for five years is a lot of time. While all my friends were happy because they thought I had been selling myself short, it was still really difficult." Ellie, twenty-seven, remembers the years after her breakup with her long-term boyfriend as one of the toughest periods of her adult life. She shares that, "The hardest part was learning how to be on my own. The loneliness really got the better of me. Plus, it was a hard time in my life—I was right out of college, I hated my job, and I missed having that cushion of someone to come home to."

Whether you are on the initiating or receiving end, the truism "breaking up is hard to do" still holds. *This American Life*, the National Public Radio show in which host Ira Glass astutely and humorously chronicles the human condition, did a segment on the anatomy of breakups and precisely pinpointed their genetic makeup.[2] Glass put it well when he said, "breaking up is a cliché you are forced to live through. It is something almost everyone is forced to endure at some point in their lives, but when it happens to you, it feels so specific."

Rob Scuka, the executive director of the National Institute of Relationship Enhancement, a nonprofit that offers relationship education for individuals and families, says that one of the more significant findings from his work with couples is that ending a relationship is difficult for both parties—perhaps more so than we even realize.[3]

Signs That It's Time to Break It Off

Let's back up for a minute. Yes, breaking up is hard, but sometimes knowing when it's time to break up is the harder part. After dating someone for a long period of time, your mind can get mushy and your perspective can get foggy. To help the clear the fog, examine the following:

- When the equation *three years invested + fear of being single = trying to stay together* is your rationale for staying together, it's probably time to walk out the door. Ask yourself: Do you really love this person, or are you using some strange relationship math that says you've gone this far, so you might as well keep going?
- Barbara Smaller, a prolific cartoonist who contributed to a book of cartoons about the lunacy of modern love, drew a cartoon with a man and woman standing next to each other and the woman asking the man, "But is really, really, really hating dating a strong enough basis for marriage?" Even if it gives you heartburn, ask yourself the same question.

- If, after a many years of dating, you still aren't sure. Yes, sometimes not knowing is knowing. Plus, ambivalence is a shaky—not to mention potentially volatile—foundation for a marriage.
- Visualize yourself married to this person a year from now. Do you imagine that you'll still have the same doubts?
- Is your standard line about the relationship, "We are going through a tough time?" Are you always in repair mode?
- Does the relationship have a pulse? Yes, the butterflies and excitement of those first few months certainly do wane, but do you still, generally, feel invested in making it work? Or is your relationship on life support? Have you stopped having sex? Has your attraction come to a raging halt?
- Do you constantly want to pick fights? On the other end of the spectrum, do you feel like communication is a lost cause?
- Have you accumulated too many grudges that you can't even imagine a scenario in which you could get over them?
- Are you not able to set your mind to enjoying your time with this person because you are so preoccupied with all the problems in your relationship?
- Are you tempted to meet, flirt, and have deep emotional and e-mail conversations with other people? Have you considered cheating?

Breaking Off an Engagement

Not all breakups are created equal. If breakups went by the homeland security color code of warnings, breaking off an engagement would be a code red. Ending an engagement used to be grounds for women to demand legal recourse. Less than a hundred years ago, until the 1930s, a woman left by her fiancé could sue for financial compensation or "damage" to her reputation under the "Breach of Promise to Marry" law. The law was meant to protect women from being seduced and left. In 2009, the "disengagement" is a much more private affair. Still, it's no less painful or jarring. But the perspective here is one offered by Michael and Harriet McManus, founders of a pro-marriage group based in Washington, D.C. called Marriage Savers, and it gets to the (broken) heart of the matter: "Better the broken engagement than a tragic divorce."[4]

Now that the calling-off of an engagement is handled, for the most part, in a less punitive fashion than it was in the earlier part of the twentieth century, you may need guidance for how to proceed when rescinding wedding invitations. People who've gone through the disengagement process said that, in addition to having emotional support, it would have been helpful to have some practical guideposts for everything from the ring (Do you give it back?), to how to break the news, to what to do with the gifts. Peggy Post, the granddaughter of the etiquette doyenne Emily Post, gives these rules for "When I Do Becomes I Don't"[5]:

- Be the first to share the news. Post says the following wording is appropriate: "Mr. and Mrs. James Hinckley announce that the marriage of their daughter Rebecca to Mr. Oliver Smith will not take place."
- Return all the gifts—and yes, this includes shower and engagement gifts as well—with a note that says something like: "Dear Jessica, I am sorry to have to tell you that Henry and I have broken our engagement. I'm returning the beautiful crystal bowl that you were so thoughtful to send. Love, Ashley."
- Don't outsource the news of the breakup to people who have been contracted for the wedding (i.e. the caterer, photographer, and band). Post says that the gold standard is to personally speak with all family and friends.
- As for the ring, Post's grandmother Emily said that it must be returned to the former fiancé. The only exception is if the ring is the bride's family heirloom.[6]

Moving Out

Jewelry, however, is not the only tangible that entangles people in a relationship—shared real estate can be just as dicey. A 2005 article in the *Christian Science Monitor* entitled "Who Loses Most in Break-Ups?" reported on a common scenario: "Everything looked promising for Lauren Laughead and her boyfriend when they moved from Boston to Dallas in 2002 for his job."[7] The picture, however, was turned less rosy when Laughead's boyfriend broke off the relationship. She then had to face the unpleasant reality of moving out (the townhouse they shared was in his name), that her credit was nonexistent because she wasn't listed on any of the bills, and that she was left with only a couch, a headboard, and a mattress—not even a bed frame. Pepper Schwartz, a professor of sociology at the University of Washington and a relationship expert for Perfect-match.com, says moving out forces couples to ask, "What do we owe each other under these circumstances—money, furniture, dogs?"[8]

In some situations, the question of who should move out is clear. For example, Jamie, discussed earlier, says, "I was breaking up with him, and he owned the apartment." As for the dog, Jamie got custody because she was more attached. She goes on to say that, "I left everything in the apartment that wasn't mine before we moved in together. I was already shaking up his world. I wanted to leave as quietly as possible." There's no one-size-fits-all solution for how to physically disentangle after a breakup, but there do seem to be some best practices. Elizabeth Kaufman, posting on a popular relationship and dating blog called The Frisky, gives some valuable suggestions in a post called "The Great Twenty-something Moveout":[9]

- Don't linger. Remember the *Sex and the City* episode when Steve, Miranda's on-and-off again boyfriend, who she later marries, continues to live with her after their breakup, and a prospective date leaves a message on Miranda's answering machine for Steve?

- Don't be there when s/he moves out.
- Do divide the stuff, but don't be petty.

The Coping Component

Breaking off a long-term relationship or getting disengaged often involves the companion activity of asking some uncomfortable questions. Sandhya, twenty-eight, says that after she broke off her three-year relationship, she couldn't help but think of those as "lost years." She says that, "I asked myself who could I have met? What could I have done? I had some regrets." It's a process that involves facing the sobering truth that the elements you need in a marriage were not in this relationship, which can lead to a windfall of disappointment. However, who feels more pain in a breakup—the breaker-upper or the breakup-ee—is not a contest or a question with a definitive answer, but feeling unwanted is definitely a tough and uncomfortable emotional state. Veronica, twenty-six, says that when her boyfriend of two years broke up with her, she found that the only thing she could really do was gradually accept it and find ways to channel her emotions: "You need to have outlets for your anger and disappointment, just keep them far away from the offending party. You will want to yell and scream and cry at the person, but this will eventually make you feel even more forlorn and unwanted. However, do whatever it takes to convince and remind yourself that you don't want or need to be with that person."

What is the consensus about whether to go cold turkey? Is it easier to take "the patch" approach and wean yourself off? Veronica, who has been through a couple of "wrenching" breakups of long-term relationships, believes that cold turkey is the best route: "There's always some slippage at first: crying phone calls, breakup sex, trying to be friends, etc., but at some point you just have to stop talking and seeing each other. You got really used to having him in your life; eventually you will get used to him not being in your life. But the separation has to happen. Maybe eventually you can be friends again, but the important thing is to acclimate to living your life without that person." Those first couple of weeks—when it feels like you are breaking a chemical addiction—can be a stinger.

Try to think about the future in small, manageable units. It's very easy to start imagining long expanses of time without the other person, thinking about the future holidays and anniversaries you won't share. This will undoubtedly make the breakup seem very overwhelming. Focus on today, this weekend—but don't go any further than that. Many former A Little Bit Marrieds say that obsessively scheduling activities so you always have a concrete list of things to look forward to is a good strategy. There's a natural tendency to look to a relationship as the thing you look forward to, as that glimmer at the end of the week.

The breakup process forces you to find a replacement for that "looking forward to" feeling. The silver-lining viewpoint is one that thinks of it as finding an upgrade.

Lisa Steadman could have a Ph.D. in breakups. After her own split, she started a blog called The Breakup Chronicles. She has found that "feelings of failure" are common, so she encourages people to see breakups through a different lens: "Society tells us that if a relationship doesn't end in marriage, you are somehow less complete as a person. But there are just some relationships that aren't for life." Cherry-picking her own best advice, Steadman suggests the following:[10]

- Give yourself credit because you are no longer in the wrong relationship.
- Create new boundaries. You have to give yourself the time and space to move on. When you talk to your ex, only discuss the issues that are necessary to discuss. And if you live together, make a list of the ways you need to begin the separation.
- Don't keep returning to the scene of the crime. Closure is an illusion. We never get all our questions answered, so don't spend too much time trying to solve the mystery of "What went wrong?"
- Get a support system in place. Chances are you are losing the person to whom you were closest, which means a backup is in order. Find at least two or three people who can be surrogates for your ex.

- Experience the stages of grief. You have to let yourself go through the denial, anger, bargaining, sadness, and acceptance.
- Your breakup didn't take your future with it. Take the focus off your ex's future and whether they are dating someone else or are happier without you, and then channel that energy into creating a vision of your own future.
- Remember how resilient you are.

What Not to Say

On the flip side, here are the worst things to say to someone who has just gotten out of a long-term relationship:

- "Now you'll never get married." This is not the time to sound alarm bells.
- "I just want to prepare you—when you get back into the dating scene, you're going to get dumped. You're going to meet a really great guy/girl and you're going to like him so much and then s/he's going to dump you."
- Anything said in the spirit of "You poor, pathetic creature . . . I pity you and I hope you don't go jump off a bridge or something." Or this variation: "I am so sorry for you. Are you okay? I'm really worried about you . . . You poor thing, our hearts are with you right now."

- "He was a d-bag." Or "she was the devil incarnate. You should have broken up with him/her three years ago." Chances are you probably still care for the person and there were reasons why your relationship lasted as long as it did, so the worst thing to hear is other people telling you that you wasted your time.

Getting Past the Fear Factor of Today's Dating Scene

Whether you decide to begin dating immediately or subscribe to the philosophy that time and living in a monastic cocoon is the healing you need to get your mojo back, you'll eventually enter the world again as a single person. Jamie goes on to describe her post-breakup approach: "After I moved out and broke up with my boyfriend of four years, I dated like crazy. I needed to see that there were other guys out there." For others, like Nitten, twenty-eight, who moved out of the apartment he and his girlfriend of over two years shared, the aftermath was less about serial dating and more about soul-searching: "I found the richness in my life again," he says, referring to how he reconnected with many of his hobbies and old friends, but then states, "Don't get me wrong though, it was still really hard."

In the post-*Sex and the City*, discredited terrorist statistic age, we know that women over forty actually have much better odds of getting married than being killed by a terrorists. At a time when singles outnumber married people, what does being a single gal look like? One storyline that emerged from the A Little Bit Marrieds was that although walking out the door is difficult, opening another one and getting back into the dating trenches is not always easy. Though part of that challenge stems from the common dating gripes—namely that it feels like a job interview with cocktails—there are psychological perceptions about being single and dating that many women encounter. Needless to say, they warrant some discussion and, in some cases, debunking. Generally, these assumptions fall under the following categories:

- I'll never meet anyone.
- Being single sucks.
- I'm going to die alone.

But none of these sentiments reflect the demographic or statistical reality. It might have seemed that the world was in dyads while you were A Little Bit Married, but singles are the fastest growing population in the country. Jillian Straus reported in a 2006 *Psychology Today* article that, "Most of us will spend more of our adult lives single than married."[11] However, even if that's the demographic reality, it still isn't stopping scores of women from having fears about never meeting anyone again. When journalist Peggy Orenstein set out to document the many facets of the modern woman's experience in her 2000 book, *Flux: Women on Sex, Work, Love, Kids and Life in a Half-Changed World*, she observed that coupling was thought of as the ultimate female achievement, noting that some have even give it holy status, calling it the Eleventh Commandment: "Thou shall not be single, over thirty, and happy."[12] Orenstein found that an overwhelming number of independent-minded women were much more fearful of being alone than of losing themselves in marriage.[13] It's interesting to note that she was writing at a cultural watershed moment when society was on the brink of shedding the social stigma associated with the single gal. *Sex and the City*, the show that transformed being a single woman into an enviable icon, was barely in its second season, and the *New York Times* was six years away from its front-page headline announcing that married people were in the minority.

Bringing Single Back

Our view of single people has changed. Thanks to a breadth of new research, books, academics, and television series, *single* now seems to have more in common with *sexy* than *spinster*. In 2006, when the terrorist statistic was found to be a misrepresentation, many articles came out in the wake of the debunking to give a more "twenty-first-century" view of singledom. Emblematic of this shift was a woman named Amy Russom, thirty-five, a manager at a San Francisco software company, though she says that even in 2006, when the *Newsweek* article in which she was quoted came out, people still routinely hit her with, "How come you're not married?" Her response is, "All I say is that I haven't met the right person yet." The new outlook, as the article synthesized it, is that, "in the years since the 'Marriage Crunch' hysteria abated, many women (and men, too) seem to have absorbed a simple, comforting mantra: if you want to get married, chances are high that sooner or later you probably will."[14]

Jane Ganahl, when she was writing the "Single Minded" column for the *San Francisco Chronicle* about unmarried life, opined that the self-pitying single girl is passé (not to mention trite), stating that, "Women who have been force fed the Bridget Jones version of single life (define yourself by the man you're with, hate yourself for being unmarried, get married at any cost) need to open their eyes."[15] Three years later, Ganahl says she is still seeing a big shift toward single people reclaiming their lives, but it's a population that needs encouragement: "I've preached to single people to stop feeling sorry for yourself, pining, and cursing the opposite sex." However, it's easy to lick your wounds when every flip of the channel has some television show that arcs around finding a mate. "You have to become impervious to those messages," says Ganahl. "Remember that making people feel at a loss is good for advertising."

Diane Mapes, a journalist and the author *How to Date in a Post-Dating World*, a tongue-in-check take on today's courtship practices, is the single woman's cheerleader: "I've never been happier living alone. I love men, have lots of male friends, and lots of great friendships." Mapes, however, did not immediately acclimate to single life. "When I got divorced and moved into my own apartment," she shares, "I was miserable. I was so lonely." But sure enough, the loneliness dissipated: "I stopped putting so much emphasis on a relationship and put more emphasis on developing myself, because then when you actually do get married, you have a lot to offer." Mary, thirty-one, who is now married but went through a thorny breakup from her boyfriend of almost three years, says she adjusted to singlehood by facing the reality that she would be fine if she never met anyone again: "I worked hard at eroding the idea that I have no worth as a person unless I have a man."

The image of single life is presented in extremes: It's either cosmos and Chanel, or cat ladies. But is this what being single really looks like? According to researcher Dr. Bella DePaulo, a psychologist and the author of *Singled Out: How Singles Are Stereotyped, Stigmatized, and Ignored, and Still Live Happily Ever After*, found that the real lives of single people are much more fulfilling than we would imagine. DePaulo argues that, "The battlefield is now psychological." She went on to say in a 2006 interview with *Psychology Today* that, "The last great way to keep women in their place is to remind them that they are incomplete. Even if you think you're happy, the messages go, you don't know real happiness."[16]

There's another component to the single narrative. Although you'll probably spend more years being single than your parents and certainly your grandparents did, the majority of us—DePaulo puts the figure at 90 percent—will get married. So with that anxiety allayed—or at least abated—maybe we can start to change the perception that marriage is Prozac and singlehood is the reason to get a prescription. "Marriage means a lot of greats things," says DePaulo. "It's a wonderful opportunity to have a rich partnership with another human being. But it's not the answer to all of your problems. Our society has advocated this intensive coupling and Jerry McGuire concept of 'you complete me.'"[17]

Of course there are great accoutrements of coupling, beyond just having a place to go for the holidays and offering a stay against loneliness. But marriage is not always a protective cocoon from loneliness. In fact, through her research DePaulo discovered that the mention of loneliness came up more from women who were unhappily coupled than from single people: "I kept hearing some version of, 'I've never felt more lonely than when I was living with my spouse and we were barely speaking.'"

Rebound Mistakes

Now that you have your psychological armor and perspective on the singles' scene, here are some common rebound mistakes culled from A Little Bit Marrieds themselves.

- Many A Little Bit Marrieds said that although the impulse might be to find the next warm body, they found they needed time before they were ready for "A Little Bit Married, take two." The conventional relationship wisdom advocates that the proportional measure of how long it takes to get over someone is six months of recovery for every year you've been together, but there's a lot of deviation there. Focus less on the exact fraction—especially now that these relationships span decades, it could be your fortieth birthday before you start dating again—and more on when you feel ready to date.

- Although his/her friends and family might have adored you, after a breakup, the troops realign with their leader. The urge might be to call his/her mother, sister, brother, or best friend in order to do some reconnaissance on what s/he's thinking, but now is the time to tap into your support system. It's painful to acknowledge that some of the people you have forged close bonds with over the past few years are now out of your inner circle, but there is little to be gained by calling on his/her college roommate or sister-in-law to coach you through the breakup.

- Be firm about not getting caught in the "dating sucks" and "I'll never meet anyone" vortex.

- As for dulling the pain, a little drinking with friends is good, but being out of control when going through strong emotional pain is not a recipe for success.

- The melting of a mock marriage is not a divorce per se, but for many it can feel like one, especially if you lived together or were engaged. But a breakup is not a failure; it's a favor to you and your unborn children. Even though the immediate aftermath can feel like you've been hit by a category-five storm, you won't always feel this way. It is good to acknowledge that breaking off a long-term relationship is a loss, one that you have to mourn in order to move on. But whether you start dating right away or take a dating hiatus, the truth is that the heart does mend itself and, in the process, often becomes more capacious.

- Finally, don't get caught up in the single spin that women over a certain age don't get married, there are no good men left, or that the universe says you are destined to be alone. That's all mental sugar. It's time to press the reset button on "How I view being single."

A Little Bit Married Rules

Ask yourself whether you are staying in the relationship because of relationship math (time invested + labor intensity of starting over = reason to stay together) or because you are making a genuine choice that this is the person you want to be with for the foreseeable future.

The party line on the disengagement is, "better a broken engagement than a tragic divorce." To handle it with aplomb, follow disengagement etiquette, which means letting your family and friends hear it from you, returning the ring (unless it was a family heirloom of yours), and returning any gifts received that are associated with the pending marriage. Think of items—such as the ring—that you've procured during the engagement as troubled assets that you want to get off your balance sheet. Same goes for the gifts.

If you are like most couples who didn't decide on the terms of a move-out before you moved in, you'll be doing some improvising. For a more graceful move-out, don't expect to stay in your house, condo, or apartment if your boyfriend/girlfriend is the owner. The codified rule is that the property owner has dibs. The move-out should happen as soon as possible. Having lingering exes on the couch is just sloppy and bad form. And spare yourself the added pain and trauma of being there when s/he moves out. Finally, don't be petty about who gets the rug that you two bought together at the market in Marrakesh.

Don't turn to your ex's support system of friends and family. "Breakup" is a euphemism for "emancipate yourself from his/her friends and family."

Being single can ratchet up a lot of fears. Try to tune out the cultural and social messages and instead adopt the radical viewpoint that not only is it fine to not be married, but also that being single has a lot of perks. And congratulations on not marrying the wrong person! On that note, remember what singles researcher DePaulo found: The loneliest segment of the population were married people living in arrangements that were riddled with tension and hostility.

8
Walking
Down the Aisle

———◆———

Lessons from Matrimony

> There is scarcely anything more difficult
> than to love one another.
>
> —Rainer Maria Rilke

We live not just in the era of A Little Bit Married, but in the era of matri-mania—two engagement parties, three bridal showers, and weddings that could cover the full cost of a college tuition. Marriage, ironically, is often glossed over in favor of lengthy discussions about color schemes, Vera or Nicole, the location of the bachelorette party, or whether to serve halibut or salmon. To coin a Hallmark card–worthy line: Weddings fade, but the marriage has to last. A common tendency among the engaged set is the "I have arrived" mentality. That is, you've arrived at your adult coming-out party and the gates of heaven will soon open and sing when you and your fiancé are pronounced "husband and wife." When you get engaged, having made it through the perilous stage of "not knowing," there's a tendency to think all the emotional heavy-lifting is over. "My work is done" you say, and now you can focus on what's really important: what type of Crate & Barrel dish sets you want, whether the bridesmaids should be allowed to pick their own shoes, and how the toile on chair should be hung. Yes, though it's a bit of an exaggeration, the point is that when many couples get engaged, they focus more on planning a wedding than building a marriage.

But what's so bad about putting a lot of time, resources, and mental energy into a day that only happens once? Well, it can eclipse more important issues that soon-to-be married couples should be mulling over. (More on that shortly.) Matrimania is insidious because it can make the wedding into the center of gravity for the relationship. In her book about the frothing of the multi-billion-dollar wedding industry, *One Perfect Day*, Rebecca Mead reported that there are now support groups for former brides who feel depressed and let down after the wedding ends. The "mania" captures how many couples think of their wedding as the peak of their relationship. Shouldn't the wedding be more like base camp? Although it's fun to think about engagement parties, wedding showers, and gift registries, don't forget about the marriage.

What Makes a Marriage

Equality

Ironically, this finding on what makes a marriage work comes from a group that only very recently has been able to legally marry: gay couples. Tara Parker-Pope broke this news in the *New York Times* in June 2008, writing, "A growing body of evidence shows that same-sex couples have a great deal to teach everyone else about marriage and relationships."[1] Despite the overplayed cultural stereotypes about bed-hopping and commitment phobia, same-sex couples are actually setting the gold standard, according to the Vermont study. Parker-Pope reported that after Vermont made same-sex unions legal in 2000, the state conducted a survey of 1,000 heterosexual and homosexual couples to look at "how their relationships were affected by common causes of marital strife, like housework, sex, and money."[2] The study found that homosexuals were far more egalitarian. Parsing out the research, she wrote, "In heterosexual couples, women did far more of the housework; men were more likely to have the financial responsibility; and men were more likely to initiate sex, while women were more likely to refuse it or to start a conversation about problems in the relationship. With same-sex couples, of course, none of these dichotomies were possible, and the partners tended to share the burdens far more equally."[3]

Imbalance in a relationship, both in terms of physical and emotional housekeeping, is exhausting, corrosive, and contempt-inducing, not to mention completely unsustainable. Couples who have broken out of the *Ozzie and Harriet* model—the television show that premiered in 1952 and became the archetype of traditional gender roles—say equality is like relationship kryptonite. Michelle Cove, a documentary filmmaker, says, "I can't really put a value on being married to someone who takes care of me as much I take care of him." Anjalie, thirty-one, says cutting loose from the prescribed gender tasks with her husband, Drew, has been their lifeline: "Gender roles were a huge concern of mine. I wasn't even sure I wanted to have kids because I didn't want to constantly be cooking and changing diapers." As an entrepreneur, Anjalie says the nonconventional arrangement—she and Drew split all the housework right down the middle—has been a crucial part to her growth in her career and has shown her that motherhood and running her own business are compatible.

An "equal relationship" isn't just a new buzz phrase or a politically correct label; it's a relationship antioxidant. Valerie Oppenheimer, a sociology professor at the University of California, Berkeley, wrote in the *Annual Review of Sociology* that a marriage based on a sharing model, in which both spouses are capable of performing economic and household work competently, is better equipped to respond to problems such as unemployment, a downturn in the economy, or the incapacitation of a spouse, than is a marriage based on strict gender specialization.[4] In *Alone Together: How Marriage in America Is Changing*, a book based on data from two studies of marital quality in America done in 1980 and 2000, four Pennsylvania State psychologists wrote that people with conservative views about gender tended to have poorer quality marriages both in 1980 as well as in 2000. The viewpoint, they found, had behavioral implications. They were associated with less marital happiness, less marital interaction, and more marital problems. And equal decision-making—defined as neither the husband nor the wife having the final word—was associated with the highest level of marital quality. Those who reported equal decision-making also reported more marital happiness, more interaction, less conflict, fewer problems, and less divorce proneness—a trend that has held for both genders.[5]

Emotional Intelligence

John Gottman is a professor of psychology at the University of Washington whose research on marriage and couples has been continuously supported by the National Institute of Mental Health. Although Gottman is not a clairvoyant, he found that he is able to predict, based on his research, with 91 percent accuracy whether a couple will stay together or divorce. Gottman writes in his book, *The Seven Principles for Making Marriage Work*, that the variable isn't intelligence, yearly income, or a degree in psychology. No, strong couples have what he calls "emotional intelligence." He states that, "They have hit upon a dynamic that keeps their negative thoughts and feelings about each other (which all couples have) from overwhelming their positive ones."[6] He also found that friendship is the determining factor for both men and women when it comes to feeling satisfied with the sex, romance, and passion in their marriage.[7]

Doing Your Marriage Homework

Have you sorted out issues about how you'll handle expenses? Are you combining bank accounts? Keeping your own but having a joint one? Have you talked about how to split holidays and deal with each other's family events and requests? Does being married now mean that you take all your vacations together and don't go out alone anymore? Have you discussed children? Are you on the same page about when—or if—you want to have them? Do you have the same baby-clock? Who is going to clean? Who is going to cook? What are your expectations, generally, surrounding how much time you'll spend together as a couple? Does one of you expect, now that you are married, you'll scale back on your sixty-hour work weeks? What is the policy about whether you are now more obligated to attend each other's events—both social and work-related—now that you've made it legal? If you haven't lived together before the wedding, have you talked about making that transition? If you have previously lived together, what will change or stay the same about your living arrangement now that you are married?

If you are getting married by a religious leader, you'll probably have some mandatory sessions with the priest or rabbi. For those who choose to go the secular route, there may not be any requirements. Regardless, it's a subject in which everyone could use more tutoring. Lucky for you, over the past few decades, the marriage preparation business has exploded with programs like PREP (Prevention and Relationship Enhancement Program). PREP was founded at the University of Denver over twenty-five years ago and its research is supported by the National Institute of Mental Health. How effective, though, can a course be? In psychologists' research on the four- and five-year follow-up PREP did with couples who took their effective communication and conflict-management skills course, there were signs that it wasn't just some pop-psychology gimmick. They compared the PREP groups with a control group and found that couples who had taken the course had higher levels of positive and lower levels of negative communications.[8] And although there is reason to be dubious of self-reporting and selection bias (people who take the course might already start with higher positives), the larger point here is one that psychologists and marriage researchers Stanley Blumberg and Mark Markman make: "Prior to the wedding day, most first time married couples have had few tests of their ability to handle conflict. They simply have not encountered many significant issues or disagreements during courtship. This is partly why satisfaction tends to be very high at this stage."[9]

There is a lack of skills out there, observes Les Parrott, who is also in the relationship skill-building business and the co-author of the international bestseller *Saving Your Marriage*

Before It Starts. He observes that, "We think we are in love and are consumed by these great conversations, so we overlook some critical skills." Parrott argues the twin engines that drive a relationship are how to resolve conflict and how to cultivate passionate intimacy when it wanes—which, unfortunately, are not innate traits. While relationship skill-building classes don't always correlate with lower divorce rates or marital satisfaction, it's worth recalling the *New York Times* headline: "Marriage Is Not Built on Surprises."

How Is Being Married Different Than Being A Little Bit Married?

Everything is the same, except some people call you "Mrs.," there are some tax breaks, and every month you put a part of your paycheck into a joint checking account. This represents one school of thought about the difference between being A Little Bit Married and married—that it's almost imperceptible. But many believe that marriage does fundamentally change your relationship. Tracey, thirty-two, says that was certainly true for her when she got married after two-and-a-half years of dating: "It's hard to describe exactly what happens when you do get married, but something shifts. We now know we are in it for the long-term, so you have a different perspective about what's important. Also, no one can leave, so you have to deal with conflict much differently than when one person can go back to his or her place."

Michaela, thirty-two, who lived with her boyfriend before they got married, says marriage is much different: "When we were a little bit married, we were more individual actors. Now we think more about our roles as husband and wife and what enacting those roles mean." Jeffrey, thirty-six, who has been married for eight years, says marriage is a lot more work than you ever think it's going to be: "There is negotiation, developing levels of understanding; it's pulling back the layers of the onion. It's a nonstop process. You have to stay very focused on making it work. Those marriage vows about for rich or for poor mean something and shape a relationship in way that I think is hard to replicate if you haven't taken them."

The Future of A Little Bit Married

Is A Little Bit Married going to become Marriage 3.0? If marriage is, as author E. J. Graff writes, for toasters, silverware, and household ware, what impetus is there to get married? Most young people today do want to get married, whether it's because they see it as an ideal ordering of a society, want to express their commitment with the highest form our culture currently offers, or for the tax breaks. A Little Bit Married is just a rite of passage, not a stasis, and it is certainly not poised to become marriage's surrogate. Most see it as ersatz to marriage— a less than ideal substitution, like NutraSweet. Whether it's at three years or a decade into the relationship, the vast majority of couples ultimately decide to walk down the aisle.

Even though there's a lot of fear percolating around getting married, and Gen Ys aren't in a rush to become Mr. and Mrs., that is not the whole complexion of this relationship stage. The vast majority of people interviewed for this book were not neutral about whether they wanted to get married. Most A Little Bit Marrieds want to, one day (to the right person), be very married. This corroborates research done by sociologists and the authors of *Alone Together*, an overview of two studies about marital trends in this country. These studies suggest that, despite the rise in cohabitation, changing gender roles, and that marriage is no longer the main event of adult life, the great majority of young adults in the United States not only have positive views of marriage, but they also wish to marry one day.[10] Lydia, twenty-seven, like many of her contemporaries, says she believes in marriage: "I don't know why, maybe because it makes it harder to break up." She adds that it's not something she wants to do during her twenties—her odyssey years—saying that, "I think marriage is really for when you are ready to settle down."

However, even if young adults aren't shunning marriage, what does prolonging the time before marriage mean for couples once they do get married? Are they better equipped to handle marriage? Or have they become hardened cynics set in their ways after spending nearly a decade in the dating trenches?

Margaret Talbot reported in *The New Yorker* on the research of two family law scholars, Naomi Cahn at George

Washington University and June Carbone at the University of Missouri at Kansas City, who are studying marriage rates in red states (defined as states that voted Republican in the 2004 president election) versus blue states (defined as states that voted Democratic). They looked at five states with the lowest median age at marriage (all red) and the five with highest median age (all blue) and found that the red-state model—marrying younger—puts couples at greater risk for divorce. Talbot explains that, "Women who marry before their mid-twenties are significantly more likely to divorce than those who marry later. And younger couples are more likely to be contending with two of the biggest stressors on a marriage: financial struggles and the birth of a baby, soon after the wedding."[11]

There are, of course, outliers. There a lot of divorces in blue states and happy marriages in red states. As Talbot synthesizes it, "Cahn and Carbone's research indicates that couples who get married later are more likely to experiment with multiple partners, postpone marriage until after they reach emotional and financial maturity, and have their children (if they have them at all) as their lives are stabilizing."[12] This confluence of factors seems to make couples less vulnerable to divorce.

Anjalie and Drew, who met after each of their thirtieth birthdays, are the poster couple for Cahn and Carbone's research. Drew relates that, "By the time we met each other, we both had it together career-wise and financially. We were more self-assured and we each knew what we wanted in a relationship because we had been through some serious trial and error."

The authors of *Alone Together* echo Cahn and Carbone, writing, "The trend for young adults to postpone marriage, therefore, may have improved the aggregate level of marital quality in the population."[13] However, they go on to add a critical caveat before jumping on the "marrying later is better" bandwagon. Their disclaimer hinges on the rise in cohabitation, which they say may have a negative impact on people's quality of life. Looking at the whole picture here, however, means that the one way to approach A Little Bit Married is to pick and choose. Think of it like a buffet: Choosing some dishes, like delaying marriage, but leaving off others, like cohabitation, might allow young people to reap the most benefits of this relationship ritual, both in the short term and the long term.

Is A Little Bit Married Beneficial for Women?

This is a difficult question. On the one hand, there are a lot of benefits for women when they delay marriage, namely giving them some crucial years to establish themselves professionally and financially. But then there is biology. For women who want to have children, there is an added dimension to delaying marriage: Women's fertility declines with age. The American Fertility Association reports that the chance of having a baby decreases 3 to 5 percent each year after a woman reaches thirty, and at a faster rate after forty.[14] That's not an antifeminist statement or a scare tactic. It's just a biological fact, which raises questions about how to take control of fertility. Cahn, the George Washington University law professor, says there are many policy solutions, one being that insurance companies need to amp up their coverage for infertility services as more women delay having children past their prime childbearing years and take a gamble with biology.

There are less desirable solutions, such as marrying a timetable, the wrong guy, or directing your 401k funds to an EFA (egg freezing account), but the bottom line is that prolonging marriage does create a different reality for women who want to have children. Discussing fertility and women's biological clocks puts you at risk of sounding glib and perpetuating the unhelpful and pressuring soundtrack of "Have babies! Your eggs are drying up." The decision of when, where, how, and why to have children is deeply personal and complex, yet it would be a vast omission to not acknowledge the impact delaying marriage has on fertility. And more than that, the question of fertility raises the original sin of A Little Bit Married—assuming and not communicating. Since women's and men's lives follow different fertility trajectories, couples in this relationship stage cannot ignore their different biology.

One interesting trend, however, is that even if it's statistically harder to conceive as you get older, a growing number of women are testing the limits of their fertility timetable. CNN reported in a piece, "Motherhood Inching Later in Life," that according to the Center for Disease Control and Prevention, more and more women are experiencing motherhood later in life. Between 2002 and 2003, birth rates for women between the ages of thirty and thirty-four increased by 4 percent, 6 percent for women thirty-five to thirty-nine, and 5 percent for women forty to forty-four.[15] Overall, according to the American Fertility Association, one in five mothers in the United States now has a first child after thirty-five.[16] Many young women today are following the lead of women like Melissa Devereaux, a mother of two who had her first child at thirty-six and her second at thirty-eight. She calls it front-loading—finding a career, traveling, and doing some solid years of due-diligence dating before settling down.

However, although front-loading works for some, it is not a one-size-fits all solution. As we continue to delay marriage, women, with the help of their partners, insurance companies, and lawmakers, will have to find ways to address this new demographic of women who are getting married later and, consequently, trying to have babies as their fertility window is closing.

A Little Bit Married Education

It's clear that A Little Bit Married is a life stage, a fact that has implications for everyone from employers who offer benefits to domestic partners, to universities that have large populations of "college marriages," to parents who often become attached and entangled in their children's mock marriages. This isn't a call for helicopter parents to start their propellers, No, hovering parents are not the solution, but neither are absent parents.

The reality of modern courtship is that many couples often find themselves isolated and ill-equipped for the transition to marriage. As Leon Kass, a University of Chicago professor who teaches a class on courtship, notes, "For the great majority, the way to the altar is uncharted territory: It's every couple on their own without a compass, often without a goal. Those who reach the altar seem to have stumbled upon it by accident."[17] But why is that? Since the time when our grandparents got married, we've seen marriage become a more private institution, siphoning our relationships off from parents, extended family, and the wider community. Robert Putman, a Harvard University sociology professor, coined the term "bowling alone" to describe the systemic decline of civic participation (his book is about the general decline of civic participation, not just exclusively tied to marriage) that's taking place across America. Now you could say we are all dating alone.

This is troubling news to many, including Virginia psychology professor Jim Coan, who believes that relationships thrive on being woven into the larger social fabric. He states that, "When I look at young people today on college campuses and think about modern courtship, the social isolation worries me." Coan says that the decline in face-to-face interaction and the transiency of the post-college years leaves many young people without a solid set of social of anchors: "My big piece of advice would be to build up networks of friends as you enter the A Little Bit Married stage of life."[18]

Many of us didn't have great role models for making the transition to marriage. Although we now have the opportunity to rewrite the marital history of our parents, that won't happen on willpower alone. The buy-in for couples to invest time, money, and energy into relationship skill-building is enormous. As a society, we need to start implementing policies and programs that go way beyond the mechanics of sexuality. Before he was president, Barack Obama wrote in *The Audacity of Hope* about marriage education workshops. He argues that,"Preliminary research shows that marriage education workshops can make a real difference in helping married couples stay together and in encouraging unmarried couples who are living together to form a more lasting bond."[19] Obama was writing, perhaps, not directly to the A Little Bit Married population, but the basics of what he suggests—more marriage and premarriage education—is where we need to head. Admittedly, the sound of government-sponsored workshops probably has about as much appeal as "Eat your peas and carrots," but this is a historical moment to think about how to create programs, both in the public and private sector, that would appeal to people in the A Little Bit Married population. As the largest generation since the Boomers head to the altar, let's think about how to keep couples out of divorce court.

They say that marriage is the most important business decision you'll ever make—an adage that has double meaning now that it's not unusual to have a wedding that could cover the down-payment of a very expensive house. But however way you slice it, walking down the aisle is a life-changing decision. Many former A Little Bit Marrieds give marriage high marks. A common echo was: "I'm surprised how much I like being married, even though it is hard work." Whether this will translate into a halving—or even quartering—of the divorce rate remains to be seen. But what we do know is that a lot remains to be done.

In the process of writing this book, I've asked myself many times: Would I get ALBM again? Being ALBM to Daniel taught me some important lessons. As for another go at it, well, given the relationship rhythms of my generation, the chances are quite high. Frankly, it's probably inevitable. What I do know for certain is that I would do it very differently the next time around. I wouldn't let ambiguity and assumptions motor the relationship. I'd deliberate more carefully about making marriage-like sacrifices and compromises. I'd have a define-the-relationship talk. I'd propose to myself. I'd be on the lookout for personality booby traps. I wouldn't ignore my doubts. I'd try to create more of a power balance in how the marriage timetable is set. I'd put issues like childcare and housework on the table. I'd talk about who brings home the bacon. I'd be careful about falling in love with potential. I'd be more aware of getting sucked into the inertia vortex. I'd keep my eyes open.

A Little Bit Married Rules

Focus less on throwing a wedding and more on building a marriage. For those of us who never had a debutante ball, a bar or bat mitzvah, or a sweet sixteen, the wedding can feel like the most defining event of your adult life. What couples often forget is that it's the marriage, not the wedding, that is the formative event taking place. With a multi-billion-dollar industry seducing couples to buy, spend, upgrade, and make the wedding the most amazing, unbelievable, super-duper tremendous day of their lives, it's easy to lose focus.

Do your marriage homework. Whether it's through the religious leader marrying you, buying books, or taking a premarriage class, you often don't know what it is that you don't know.

Relationship education needs to continue beyond the condom-on-the-cucumber demonstration, which is the last form of relationship education most of us receive. Parents, political leaders, educators, and other organizations should start a dialogue with young people moving through this relationship stage in order to provide guidance on how to make the transition to marriage. To be clear, this is not a call-to-arms for a pro-marriage movement or a didactic series of workshops touting the benefits of marriage. Rather, it's an opportunity to think about some creative and innovative ways to help this generation build stronger relationships and marriages.

Meet the Interviewed

A Little Bit Married started with a big question: How do you navigate the now most common romantic rite of passage and modern courtship? To answer it required drawing on expertise from psychologists, sociologists, journalists, and relationship experts. Although they've all been credentialed in the book, those are only snippets of the breadth and depth of their accomplishments and research. Here's a proper introduction.

Jeffrey Arnett is a research professor in the Department of Psychology at Clark University in Worcester, Massachusetts.

Along with numerous scholarly articles in this area, he also coined the term "emerging adulthood" when he authored the book *Emerging Adulthood: The Winding Road from the Late Teens Through the Twenties.* He is also the author of the textbook *Adolescence and Emerging Adulthood: A Cultural Approach.* In 2005, he was a Fulbright Scholar at the University of Copenhagen, Denmark. Since 2002, he has served as editor of the *Journal of Adolescent Research.* Please visit www.jeffreyarnett.com to learn more.

Robert A. Burton, M.D., graduated from Yale University and the University of California at San Francisco medical school, where he also completed his neurology residency. At age thirty-three, he was appointed chief of the Division of Neurology at Mt. Zion–UCSF Hospital, where he subsequently became Associate Chief of the Department of Neurosciences. His non-neurology writing career includes the recent book, *On Being Certain: Belieiving You Are Right Even When You're Not,* several critically acclaimed novels and a neuroscience and culture column, Mind Reader, at Salon.com. He lives in the San Francisco Bay Area.

Neil Chethik is an author, speaker, and expert specializing in men's lives and family issues. He is the author of *VoiceMale: What Husbands Really Think About Their Marriages, Their Wives, Sex, Housework and Commitment* and *Fatherloss: How Sons of All Ages Come To Terms With the Deaths of Their Dads.* Previously, Neil was a staff reporter for the *Tallahassee Democ-*

rat and *San Jose Mercury News*, and writer of "VoiceMale," the first syndicated column on men's personal lives. His writings have appeared in hundreds of print and Web publications. Please visit www.neilchethik.com to learn more.

Jim Coan is director of the Virginia Affective Neuroscience Laboratory and assistant professor of psychology at the University of Virginia. His work emphasizes the neural mechanisms underlying emotional expression, emotion regulation, and social relationships. His recent focus has been on how the brain transforms social soothing and proximity into better health and well-being.

Stephanie Coontz is a professor of history and family studies at The Evergreen State College in Olympia, Washington, and is director of research and public education for the Council on Contemporary Families, which she chaired from 2001 to 2004. She is the author of *Marriage, A History: How Love Conquered Marriage*, *The Way We Never Were: American Families and the Nostalgia Trap*, *The Way We Really Are: Coming to Terms with America's Changing Families*, and *The Social Origins of Private Life: A History of American Families*. She has appeared on the *Today* show, the *Oprah Winfrey* show, NPR, and *MSNBC with Brian Williams*, among others. Her work has been featured in publications such as the *New York Times*, the *Observer/Guardian*, *Wall Street Journal*, *Salon*, *Washington Post*, *Newsweek*, *Harper's*, and *Vogue*. Please visit www.stephanie coontz.com to learn more.

Michelle Cove is the coauthor of national bestseller *I'm Not Mad, I Just Hate You!: A New Understanding of Mother-Daughter Conflict*. Ms. Cove is the creator of the documentary *Seeking Happily Ever After*, which is aimed at challenging women's perceptions of being single. Please visit www.seekinghappily everafter.com to learn more.

Gary Cross is a Distinguished Professor of modern history at Penn State University. He focuses on consumption, childhood, and leisure issues. Most recently, he is the author of *Men to Boys: The Making of Modern Immaturity* and *All-Consuming Century: Why Commercialism Won in Modern America*.

Bella DePaulo has a Ph.D. in psychology from Harvard and is the author of *Singled Out: How Singles Are Stereotyped, Stigmatized, and Ignored, and Still Live Happily Ever After*. She also writes the "Living Single" blog for *Psychology Today*. Dr. DePaulo has appeared on the *Today* show, CNN, and ABC. Her op-eds have appeared in the *New York Times*, the *Chronicle of Higher Education*, and the *San Francisco Chronicle*. Please visit www.belladepaulo.com to learn more.

Helen E. Fisher, Ph.D., is research professor and member of the Center for Human Evolutionary Studies in the Department of Anthropology at Rutgers University. She has conducted extensive research on the evolution and future of human sex, love, marriage, and gender differences in the brain and behavior. She has written five books. Her most recent is

Why Him? Why Her?: Finding Real Love By Understanding Your Personality Type. Ms. Fisher is currently chief scientific advisor to Chemistry.com, where she has collaborated in the development of their Chemistry Profile™ personality assessment and matching system. Please visit www.helenfisher.com to learn more.

Jane Ganahl has been a journalist, editor, author, consultant, and community organizer in San Francisco for twenty-five years. She is the author of the novelized memoir, *Naked on the Page: The Misadventures of My Unmarried Midlife*, which has been optioned for a TV series by TBS. For almost five years she wrote "Single Minded," a Sunday column about the unmarried life, for the *San Francisco Chronicle*. Ms. Ganahl's work has appeared in the *Huffington Post*, Salon.com, and *Rolling Stone*. Please visit www.janeganahl.com to learn more.

Kathleen Gerson is professor of sociology at New York University and the 2008–2009 president of the Eastern Sociological Society. She has held visiting positions at the Russell Sage Foundation and the Center for the Study of Status Passages, among many others. The author and coauthor of five books and numerous articles, Gerson's work has focused on the connections among gender, work, and family life in postindustrial America.

Kay S. Hymowitz is the William E. Simon Fellow at the Manhattan Institute and a contributing editor of *City Journal*.

She writes extensively on education and childhood in America. Ms. Hymowitz is the author of *Marriage and Caste in America: Separate and Unequal Families in a Post-Marital Age*, a compilation of some of her previously published *City Journal* essays. Ms. Hymowitz has also written for many major publications, including the *New York Times*, the *Washington Post*, the *Wall Street Journal*, *The New Republic*, *New York Newsday*, *The Public Interest*, *Commentary*, *Dissent*, and *Tikkun*.

Michael Kimmel is among the leading researchers and writers on men and masculinity in the world today. His most recent book is called *Guyland: Understanding The Perilous World Where Boys Become Men*. He is a professor of sociology and gender studies at State University of New York, Stony Brook. Please visit www.guyland.net to learn more.

Dr. Diana Kirschner is a psychologist and author of *Love in 90 Days: The Essential Guide to Finding Your Own True Love*. Dr. Kirschner ran the Institute for Comprehensive Family Therapy, a nationally recognized, post-graduate center devoted to training psychiatrists, psychologists, and therapists. As part of that training, she did "live" breakthrough sessions with singles, couples, and families who were stuck at an impasse in therapy. Please visit www.lovein90days.com to learn more.

Cooper Lawrence is a relationship and psychology expert with a master's degree in developmental psychology. She is currently finishing her doctorate in applied developmental psychology. She is the host of her own nationally syndicated radio show, *The Cooper Lawrence Show*. Ms. Lawrence is the author of four books, her most recent being *The Cult Of Perfection: Make Peace With Your Inner Overachiever.* Please visit www.cooperlawrence.com to learn more.

Diane Mapes has written essays on pop culture, the single life, television, travel, naked sushi, and more for publications such as *Bust*, *Health*, the *Los Angeles Times*, the *Washington Post*, and the recent anthology *Single Women of a Certain Age.* Her popular essays about dating appear in the *Seattle Times* and were the springboard for *How to Date in a Post-Dating World*, a humorous look at today's courtship practices. Please visit www.dianemapes.net to learn more.

Dr. Amanda Miller is an assistant professor of sociology at the University of Central Oklahoma where she teaches courses in social stratification and human services. Her research focuses primarily on family change including trends in fertility, union transitions, and the ways that couples do gender within cohabiting relationships. She received her Ph.D. in sociology from The Ohio State University. Her dissertation topic was: Playing House? The Paid Work and Domestic Divisions of Working Class, Class-Straddling, and Middle Class Cohabiting Couples.

Marshall Miller and Dorian Solot founded the Alternatives to Marriage Project in 1998. They are the authors of

Unmarried to Each Other: The Essential Guide to Living Together as an Unmarried Couple, a guidebook for unmarried couples of all sexual orientations. They currently tour college campuses as sex educators. Please visit www.unmarried.org to learn more.

Les Parrott is a professor of psychology at Seattle Pacific University and the author of the bestselling book *Saving Your Marriage Before It Starts*. He founded the Center for Relationship Development on the campus of Seattle Pacific University. In addition, he is a Fellow in medical psychology at the University of Washington School of Medicine. He has been featured in media outlets such as *Good Morning America*, the *Oprah Winfrey* show, and 20/20.

Esther Perel is a licensed marriage and family therapist. She is the author of the international bestseller *Mating in Captivity: Unlocking Erotic Intelligence*. She has written numerous articles and chapters about intermarriage, the families of Holocaust survivors, cross-cultural couples and cultural and religious identity, and sexuality. Please visit www.estherperel.com to learn more.

Sharon Sassler, Ph.D., is a social demographer at Cornell University. Her research examines factors shaping the activities of young adults and their life-course transitions into school and work, relationships, and parenthood. Her work focuses on how these transitions vary by gender, race/ethnicity, and class. Some of her current projects examine the processes underlying entrance into cohabiting unions and the meaning cohabiters assign to their unions.

Pamela Smock is a research professor in the Population Studies Center at the University of Michigan. She also holds appointments in the sociology and women's studies departments. She specializes in the study of family, gender, and social inequality. Of particular interest for her are gender inequality, changing family patterns, and the implications of each for the other. Her research has focused on the economic consequences of divorce and marriage, nonresident fatherhood, remarriage, single-mother families, child support, and unmarried cohabitation. Currently, she is examining racial, ethnic, and gender variation in the meaning and implications of cohabitation in the United States.

Scott Stanley, Ph.D., is codirector of the Center for Marital and Family Studies and a research professor of psychology at the University of Denver. He has authored numerous research articles on relationships and is an expert on marital commitment. Dr. Stanley coauthored the book *Fighting for Your Marriage* and developed video and audio tapes by the same title. He is also the coauthor of *A Lasting Promise* and author of *The Heart of Commitment* and *The Power of Commitment*. Additionally, he regularly contributes to print and broadcast media as an expert on marriage.

Lisa Steadman is the author of *It's a Breakup, Not a Breakdown*, which is the result of her in-depth study and understanding of breakups, dating, and relationships. Please visit www.lisa steadman.com to learn more.

Laura Sessions Stepp is a journalist specializing in the coverage of young people and sexuality. She is the author of *Unhooked: How Young Women Pursue Sex, Delay Love, and Lose at Both*. Ms. Stepp has written about children and families for more than fifteen years and is a frequent public speaker around the country. Her work has appeared in publications such as the *Washington Post*, *Parent*, *Child*, *Working Mother*, and *Reader's Digest*. She served as a member of a panel on adolescence for the U.S. Surgeon General and sits on the board of advisors of the Casey Journalism Center for Children and Families at the University of Maryland. Please visit www.laurastepp.com to learn more.

Jean M. Twenge, Ph.D., is associate professor of psychology at San Diego State University and the author of more than forty scientific journal articles and book chapters. Her book, *Generation Me: Why Today's Young Americans Are More Confident, Assertive, Entitled—and More Miserable Than Ever Before*, uses data from 1.3 million young people to show the real differences between generations on issues like self-esteem, individualism, anxiety, and sexuality. Her most recent book, *The Narcissism Epidemic: Living in the Age of Entitlement*, was published in April 2009. Please visit www.jeantwenge.com to learn more.

Linda Waite is the Lucy Flower Professor in urban sociology at the University of Chicago. She is the author of many books, including *The Case for Marriage: Why Married People Are Happier, Healthier, and Better Off Financially*. Waite's current research interests include social demography, aging, the family, health, working families, and the link between biology, psychology, and the social world.

Sarah Whitton received her Ph.D. in 2004 from the University of Denver. Then, at Harvard Medical School and Judge Baker Children's Center, she completed a two-year postdoctoral fellowship in the clinical research training program. Her primary research interests focus on how close relationships, especially those between spouses and between parents and children, influence and are influenced by the individuals' mental health.

Acknowledgments

This book has the DNA and handprints of many people. First and foremost, thank you to the interviewees—the hundreds of A Little Bit Marrieds who let me into their inner lives and gave the coordinates to map this relationship stage. You all are the backbone of this book. A huge debt of gratitude to Elisabeth Weed, my agent, who took a chance on me when I only had one clip from the *Gay City News*. Thank you so much to Alice Peck for being the ultimate sounding board and my rabbi on everything writing-related. Many thanks to Katie McHugh at Da Capo for your incisive editing and belief in this project from the very beginning.

Thank you to Jamie Kaufman for not only providing material, but the kind of perspective I'd like to bottle and sell. I'm enormously grateful to Brie Walsh for the personal and professional support throughout the years. Thank you to Colleen Cary for turning so many bad dates in to much more interesting conversations about human psychology. Thank you to Brooke Moorhead for, again, being such an excellent guinea pig. Thank you to Andrew Eil for his nimble mind, ability to see the hole in any argument, and constant encouragement.

A very special thank you to my grandmother, Gloria Schaffer, for her continued musings and thoughts on modern courtship. Thanks to my grandfather, David Seligson, the medical miracle, who, at ninety-three, is a model of astuteness.

Thank you to my father, Stephen Schaffer, for his sense of humor, unconventional insights, and love.

Notes

Notes to Introduction

1. "Prince William's Romance Renewed? Signs Point to a Reunion with Kate Middleton and, Perhaps, Wedding Bells in '09" CBS via *ShowBuzz*, July 9, 2007, http://www.showbuzz.cbsnews.com/stories/2007/07/09/people_royalty/main3030765.shtml.

Notes to Chapter 1

1. David Brooks, "The Odyssey Years," *New York Times,* October 9, 2007, http://select.nytimes.com/2007/10/09/opinion/10brooks.html.

2. Interview with Michael Kimmel.

3. Stephanie Rosenbloom, "A Disconnect On Hooking Up," *New York Times,* March 1, 2007, http://www.nytimes.com/2007/03/01/fashion/01hook.html.

4. Laura Sessions Stepp, "In Spring '06, a Young Man's Fancy Turns to Work . . . ," *The Washington Post,* March 26, 2006, http://www.washingtonpost.com/wp-dyn/content/article/2006/03/25/AR2006032500839.html.

5. *Mary Madden* and *Amanda Lenhart,* "Online Dating Report," Pew Internet & American Life Project, March 5, 2006, p.19, http://www.pewinternet.org/PPF/r/177/report_display.asp.

6. Tamala Edwards, "Who Needs a Husband?" *Time* magazine, July 5, 2007, http://www.time.com/time/magazine/article/0,9171,997804,00.html.

7. U.S. Census Bureau Internet Press Release, September 21, 2006, http://www.census.gov/population/socdemo/hh-fam/ms2.pdf.

8. Nancy Wartik, "The Perils of Playing House," *Psychology Today,* July/August 2005, http://psychologytoday.com/articles/200506/the-perils-of-playing-house.

9. Kimberly Hayes Taylor, "Shacking Up," *The Detroit News,* October 2, 2005, http://www.detnews.com/2005/editorial/0510/02/A17–334044.htm.

10. Interview with Helen Fisher.

11. Interview with Kathleen Gerson.

12. Alex Kuczynski, "NOTICED: Between the Sexes, It's World War III Out There," *New York Times,* July 19, 1998, http://www.nytimes.com/1998/07/19/style/noticed-between-the-sexes-it-s-world-war-iii-out-there.html.

13. Barbara DaFoe Whitehead, "The Plight of the High Status Woman," *Atlantic Monthly,* December 1999, v. 284, n. 6, pp. 120–124.

14. Interview with Esther Perel.

15. Ibid.

16. Greenberg Quinlan Rosner, "Coming of Age in America, Part II," September 2005, http://www.greenbergresearch.com/index.php?ID=1659. The survey sample is a nationally representative Internet sample, created by matching Polimetrix panelists to demographic characteristics among randomly selected records of eighteen-to twenty-four-year olds in the 2004 American Community Survey (ACS) dataset.

Notes to Chapter 2

1. David Grosz, "A Final Kiss Before Growing Up," *The New York Sun,* September 15, 2006, http://www.nysun.com/arts/final-kiss-before-growing-up/39774/.

2. Kay Hymowitz, "Child-Man in the Promised Land," *City Journal*, Winter 2008, vol. 18 no. 1, http://www.city-journal.org/2008/18_1_single_young_men.html.

3. *Linda J. Waite, The Ties that Bind: Perspectives on Marriage and Cohabitation*, Aldine de Gruyter: New York, 2000, p. 7.

4. Meghan O'Rourke, "Diamonds Are a Girl's Worst Friend," Slate.com, June 11, 2007, http://www.slate.com/id/2167870/.

5. Interview with Stephanie Coontz.

6. Michael Kimmel, *Guyland: The Perilous World Where Boys Become Men*, HarperCollins: New York,2008, p. 9.

7. Hal R. Varian, "Analyzing the Marriage Gap," *New York Times,* July 29, 2004, http://people.ischool.berkeley.edu/~hal/people/hal/NYTimes/2004-07-29.html.

8. Scott Stanley, "What Is It with Men and Commitment, Anyway?" Keynote Address to the Sixth Annual Smart Marriages Conference, Washington, D.C., July 2002, http://www.smartmarrieages.com/stanley.men.anyway.html.

9. Barbara Dafoe Whitehead and David Popenoe, *The Social Health of Marriage in America 2004*, essay: "The Marrying Kind: Which Men Marry and Why," http://marriage.rutgers.edu/Publications/SOOU/TEXTSOOU2004.htm.

10. David Crary, "Study: Majority of Men Do Want to Get married," *Associated Press*, June 23, 2004, http://www.azcentral.com/families/articles/0623menand marriage-ON.html.

11. Interview with Michael Kimmel.

12. Interview with Neil Chethik.

13. Interview with Gary Cross.

Notes to Chapter 3

1. Interview with Sarah Whitton.

2. Kathleen Gerson, "What Do Women and Men Want?" *The American Prospect,* February 19, 2007, http://www.prospect.org/cs/articles?articleId=12499.

3. Ibid.

4. Eric V. Copage, "Marriage Is Not Built on Surprises, *New York Times*, December 17, 2006, http://www.nytimes.com/2006/12/17/fashion/weddings/17field.html.

5. Ibid.

Notes to Chapter 4

1. Sam Roberts, "To Be Married Means to Be Outnumbered," *New York Times*, October 15, 2006, http://www.nytimes.com/2006/10/15/us/15census.html.

2. Kimberly Hayes Taylor, "Shacking Up: More Couples Say Yes to Sharing Homes, No to Marriage: Is that a Problem?" *The Detroit News*, October 2, 2005, http://www.detnews.com/2005/editorial/0510/02/A17–334044.htm.

3. Roberts.

4. Interview with Pamela Smock.

5. Pamela Smock, "Cohabitation in the United States: An Appraisal of Research Themes, Findings, and Implications," *Annual Review of Sociology*, 2000, vol. 26, pp. 1–20.

6. Ibid.

7. Ibid.

8. Ibid.

9. Larry Bumpass and Hsien-Hen Lu, "Trends in Cohabitation and Implications for Children's Family Contexts in the United States," *Population Studies*, 2000, v. 54, pp. 29–41.

10. Interview with Sharon Sassler.

11. Sharon Jayson, "Living Together No Longer 'Playing House'," USA Today, July 28, 2008, http://www.usatoday.com/news/health/2008–07–28-cohabitation -research_N.htm.

12. Ibid.

13. Interview with Marshall Miller.

14. Interview with Linda Waite.

15. Interview with Pamela Smock.

16. Interview with Sharon Sassler.

17. David Popenoe and Barbara Dafoe Whitehead, Should We Live Together? What Young Adults Need to Know about Cohabitation before Marriage, The National Marriage

Project at Rutgers University, 2nd ed., http://marriage.rutgers.edu/Publica tions/SWLT2%20TEXT.htm.

18. Sascha Rothschild, "How to Get Divorced by 30," *LA Weekly*, March 26, 2008, http://www.laweekly.com/la-vida/la-vida/how-to-get-divorced-by-30/18574/ ?page=3.

19. Taylor.

20. Devin Sipher, "Vows: Nicola Kraus and David Wheir," *New York Times*, July 6, 2008, http://www.nytimes.com/2008/07/06/fashion/weddings/06vows.html.

21. Scott Stanley, "What Is It with Men and Commitment, Anyway?" Keynote Address to the Sixth Annual Smart Marriages Conference, Washington D.C., July 2002, http://www.smartmarriages.com/stanley.men.anyway.html.

22. Interview with Pamela Smock.

23. Clay Risen, "Cohabitation Is Bad for Women's Health," *New York Times Magazine*, December 10, 2006, http://www.nytimes.com/2006/12/10/magazine/10section1B.t-1.html.

24. G. K. Rhoades, S. M. Stanley, and H. J. Markman, "Pre-engagement Cohabitation and Gender Asymmetry in Marital Commitment," *Journal of Family Psychology*, 2006, vol. 20, 553–560.

25. Interview with Sharon Sassler.

26. Sharon Jayson, "Real Break-ups? Not So Funny," *USA Today*, June 5, 2006, http://www.usatoday.com/news/health/2006–06–05-break-ups_x.htm.

27. Interview with Amanda Miller.

28. Cathi Hanauer, ed., *The Bitch In the House: 26 Women Tell the Truth About Sex, Solitude, Work, Motherhood, and Marriage*, HarperCollins: New York, 2002, p. 20.

Notes to Chapter 5

1. "What Do Women Want?" Meredith and NBC Universal poll, July 2008, http://www.whatdowomenwantstudy.com/, http://www.marketingcharts.com/topics/demographics/women-happy-overall-want-more-help-at-home-and-better-sex-5529/meredith-nbc-universal-what-women-want-women-priorities-generation-july-2008jpg/.

2. Greenberg Quinlan Rosner, "Coming of Age in America, Part II," September 2005. http://www.greenbergresearch.com/index.php?ID=1659. The survey sample is a nationally representative Internet sample, created by matching Polimetrix panelists to demographic characteristics among randomly selected records of eighteen-to-twenty-four year olds in the 2004 American Community Survey (ACS) dataset.

3. Kamy Wicoff, *I Do But I Don't*, Da Capo Press: Cambridge, MA, 2006, p. 23.

4. Interview with Michael Kimmel.

5. Rebecca Mead, *One Perfect Day: The Selling of the American Wedding*, Penguin Press: New York, 2007, p. 29.

6. Jane Ganahl, "Should She Follow the Man or the Job?," *San Francisco Chronicle*, April 23, 2006, http://www.sfgate.com/cgi-bin/article.cgi?f=/c/a/2006/04/23/LVG1GIAG0C1.DTL.

7. Lisa Belkin, "Your Old Man," *New York Times Magazine*, April 1, 2009, http://www.nytimes.com/2009/04/05/magazine/05wwln-lede-t.html.

8. Interview with Sarah Whitton.

9. Jennifer D'Angelo, "Experts Reveal: How to Get Your Man to Propose," FoxNews.com, May, 13, 2005, http://www.foxnews.com/story10,2933,156404,00 .html.

10. Interview with Neil Chethik.

Notes to Chapter 6

1. "Divorce Rates," Divorce Statistics Collection, Americans for Divorce Reform, http://www.divorcereform.org/rates.html.

2. Joann Klimkiewicz, "Are Modern Standards Too High?," *Hartford Courant*, February 15, 2007, http://www.courant.com/features/lifestyle/hc-expectations.art feb15,0,1396359,print.story.

3. Barbara Dafoe Whitehead and David Popenoe, "The State of our Unions: The Social Health of Marriage in America 2001," The National Marriage Project at Rutgers University, http://marriage.rutgers.edu/Publications/SOOU/TEXT SOOU2001.htm.

4. Klimkiewicz.

5. Interview with Jeffrey Arnett.

6. Stephanie Coontz, "Too Close For Comfort," *New York Times*, November 7, 2006, http://select.nytimes.com/search/restricted/article?res=F30A1FF83A5 B0C748CDDA80994DE404482.

7. Charles Darwin, "This is the Question," from The Complete Works of Charles Darwin Online, http://darwin-online.org.uk/content/frameset?viewtype= text&itemID=CUL-DAR210.8.2&pageseq=1.

Hannah Seligson, "The Science of When to Get Married," *The Daily Beast*, April 7, 2009, http://www.thedailybeast.com/blogs-and-stories/2009-04-07/ the-science-of-when-to-get-married/full/.

8. Interview with Jean Twenge.

9. Daniel B Wile, *After the Honeymoon: How Conflict Can Improve Your Relationship*, John Wiley & Sons: New York, 1988, p. 12.

10. Robert Burton, On Being Certain: Believing You Are Right Even When You're Not, St Martin's Press: New York, 2008, p. xi.

11. Ibid., p. 223.

12. Interview with Robert Burton.

13. "What's Love Got to Do With It: Long Term Study Reveals What Makes Some Marriages Last," http://www.utexas.edu/features/archive/2003/love.html.

14. Interview with Diana Kirschner.

15. Interview with Jim Coan.

16. John M. Gottman, Ph.D., and Nan Silver, *The Seven Principles for Making Marriage Work: A Practical Guide from the Country's Foremost Relationship Expert,* Three Rivers Press: New York, 1999, p. 31.

17. David H. Olson and Amy K. Olson, *Empowering Couples Building on Your Strengths,* Life Innovations, Inc., February, 2000, p. 9.

18. Ibid., p. 53.

19. "What's Love Got to Do With It: Long Term Study Reveals What Makes Some Marriages Last," http://www.utexas.edu/features/archive/2003/love.html.

20. Judy Brady, "Why I Want a Wife," *Ms. Magazine,* Spring 1972, http://www.joanbrady.co.uk/assets_cm/files/PDF/why_i_want_a_wife.pdf

21. Marilyn Yalom, A History of the Wife, HarperCollins, New York, 2001, p. 400.

22. Ibid.

23. Interview with Les Parrott.

24. Maureen Dowd, "An Ideal Husband," *New York Times*, July 6, 2008, http://www.nytimes.com/2008/07/06/opinion/06dowd.html.

Notes to Chapter 7

1. Sharon Jayson, "Real Break-ups? Not So Funny," *USA Today*, June 5th, 2006, http://www.usatoday.com/news/health/2006–06–05-break-ups_x.htm.

2. *This American Life*, National Public Radio, Episode 339: "Break-up," August 15, 2008, http://www.thisamericanlife.org/Radio_Episode.aspx?episode=339.

3. Interview with Rob Scuka.

4. Rachel Safier with Wendy Roberts, *There Goes the Bride: Making Up Your Mind, Calling It Off, And Moving On*, Wiley: San Francisco, 2003, p. xi.

5. "Engagement Break-ups: When 'I Do' Becomes 'I Don't,'" Wedding Channel.com, August 28, 2008, http://www.celebrityweddingbuzz.com/celebrity_weddings/2008/08/on-tuesday-desp.html.

6. Ibid.

7. Marilyn Gardner, "Who Loses Most in Breakups?" *The Christian Science Monitor*, May 18, 2005, http://www.csmonitor.com/2005/0518/p11s01-lifp.html.

8. Ibid.

9. Elizabeth Kaufman, "The Great Twenty-Something Moveout," July 7th, 2008, http://www.thefrisky.com/post/246-first-time-for-everything-the-great-twenty something-move-out/.

10. Interview with Lisa Steadman.

11. Jillian Straus, "Lone Stars: Being Single," *Psychology Today*, May/June 2006, http://psychologytoday.com/articles/pto-20060424–000003.xml.

12. Peggy Orenstein, *Flux: Women on Sex, Work, Love, Kids, and Life in a Half-Changed World*, Anchor Books: New York, 2000, p. 241.

13. Ibid., pp. 30, 21.

14. Daniel McGinn, "Marriage by the Numbers," *Newsweek*, June 5, 2006 http://www.msnbc.msn.com/id/13007828/site/newsweek/page/2/.

15. Jane Ganahl, "Dear Diary: Bridget Jones Had it All Wrong," *San Francisco Chronicle*, September 11, 2005, http://www.sfgate.com/cgibin/article.cgi?file=/c/a/2005/09/11/LVGB0EHL941.DTL.

16. Ibid.

17. Interview with Bella DePaulo.

Notes to Chapter 8

1. Tara Parker-Pope, "Gay Unions Shed Light on Gender in Marriage," *New York Times*, June 10, 2008, http://www.nytimes.com/2008/06/10/health/10well.html.

2. Ibid.

3. Ibid.

4. Paul R. Amato, Alan Booth, David R. Johnson, and Stacy J. Rogers, *Alone Together: How Marriage in America Is Changing*, Harvard University Press: Cambridge, MA, 2007, p. 27.

5. Amato et al., pp. 167, 170.

6. John M. Gottman and Nan Silver, *The Seven Principles for Making Marriage Work: A Practical Guide from the Country's Foremost Relationship Expert*, Three Rivers Press: New York, 1999, p. 3.

7. Gottman and Silver, p. 10.

8. H. J. Markman, M. J. Renick, F. Floyd, S. Stanley, and M. Clements, "Preventing Marital Distress Through Communication and Conflict Management Training: A Four and Five Year Follow-up," *Journal of Consulting and Clinical Psychology*, 1993, vol. 62, pp. 70–77.

9. *Rony Berger and Mo Therese Hannah, Preventive Approaches in Couples Therapy*, Brunner/Mazel: Philadelphia, PA, 1999, p. 282.

10. Amato et al., p. 2.

11. Margaret Talbot, "Red Sex Blue Sex," *New Yorker*, November 3, 2008, pp. 66–67.

12. Ibid.

13. Amato et al., p. 20.

14. The American Fertility Association, http://www.theafa.org/library/article/age_and_female_fertility/.

15. Lauren Gracco, "Motherhood Inching Later in Life," CNN.com, May 7, 2005, http://edition.cnn.com/2005/HEALTH/parenting/05/06/motherhood/index.html.

16. The American Fertility Association.

17. Leon R. Kass, "The End of Courtship," Boundless.org, October 13, 2005, http://www.boundless.org/2005/articles/a0001154.cfm.

18. Interview with Jim Coan.

19. Barack Obama, *The Audacity of Hope: Thoughts on Reclaiming the American Dream* Vintage: New York, 2008, p. 394.

Index

Index entries referring to the phrase "A Little Bit Married"
are denoted by the abbreviation ALBM.